OPPOSING VIEWPOINTS® SERIES

P9-CJK-021

Education

Other Books of Related Interest:

Opposing Viewpoints Series
School Policies

At Issue Series
Has No Child Left Behind Been Good for Education?
Has Technology Increased Learning?
Year Round Schools

Current Controversies Series
Homeschooling

"Congress shall make no law . . . abridging the freedom of speech, or of the press."

First Amendment to the U.S. Constitution

The basic foundation of our democracy is the First Amendment guarantee of freedom of expression. The Opposing Viewpoints Series is dedicated to the concept of this basic freedom and the idea that it is more important to practice it than to enshrine it.

OPPOSING VIEWPOINTS® SERIES

| Education

David Haugen and Susan Musser, Book Editor

GREENHAVEN PRESS
A part of Gale, Cengage Learning

GALE
CENGAGE Learning

Detroit • New York • San Francisco • New Haven, Conn • Waterville, Maine • London

GALE
CENGAGE Learning

Christine Nasso, *Publisher*
Elizabeth Des Chenes, *Managing Editor*

© 2009 Greenhaven Press, a part of Gale, Cengage Learning.

Gale and Greenhaven Press are registered trademarks used herein under license.

For more information, contact:
Greenhaven Press
27500 Drake Rd.
Farmington Hills, MI 48331-3535
Or you can visit our Internet site at gale.cengage.com

For product information and technology assistance, contact us at

Gale Customer Support, 1-800-877-4253
For permission to use material from this text or product, submit all requests online at www.cengage.com/permissions

Further permissions questions can be emailed to permissionrequest@cengage.com

Articles in Greenhaven Press anthologies are often edited for length to meet page requirements. In addition, original titles of these works are changed to clearly present the main thesis and to explicitly indicate the author's opinion. Every effort is made to ensure that Greenhaven Press accurately reflects the original intent of the authors. Every effort has been made to trace the owners of copyrighted material.

Cover photograph reproduced by permission of Millan/Dreamstime.com.

LIBRARY OF CONGRESS CATALOGING-IN-PUBLICATION DATA

Education / David Haugen and Susan Musser.
    p. cm. -- (Opposing viewpoints)
    Includes bibliographical references and index.
    ISBN-13: 978-0-7377-4208-4 (hardcover)
    ISBN-13: 978-0-7377-4209-1 (pbk.)
    1. Public schools--United States. 2. Privatization in education--United States. 3. Religion in the public schools--United States. 4. Moral education--United States. I. Haugen, David M., 1969- II. Musser, Susan.
    LA217.2.E34 2009
    370.973--dc22
                                                      2008031458

Printed in the United States of America
1 2 3 4 5 6 7 12 11 10 09 08

Contents

Chapter 3: Should Religious and Moral Values Be Taught as Part of Public Education?

Chapter 4: How Should the Education System Be Improved?

Why Consider Opposing Viewpoints?

> "The only way in which a human being can make some approach to knowing the whole of a subject is by hearing what can be said about it by persons of every variety of opinion and studying all modes in which it can be looked at by every character of mind. No wise man ever acquired his wisdom in any mode but this."
>
> *John Stuart Mill*

In our media-intensive culture it is not difficult to find differing opinions. Thousands of newspapers and magazines and dozens of radio and television talk shows resound with differing points of view. The difficulty lies in deciding which opinion to agree with and which "experts" seem the most credible. The more inundated we become with differing opinions and claims, the more essential it is to hone critical reading and thinking skills to evaluate these ideas. Opposing Viewpoints books address this problem directly by presenting stimulating debates that can be used to enhance and teach these skills. The varied opinions contained in each book examine many different aspects of a single issue. While examining these conveniently edited opposing views, readers can develop critical thinking skills such as the ability to compare and contrast authors' credibility, facts, argumentation styles, use of persuasive techniques, and other stylistic tools. In short, the Opposing Viewpoints Series is an ideal way to attain the higher-level thinking and reading skills so essential in a culture of diverse and contradictory opinions.

In addition to providing a tool for critical thinking, Opposing Viewpoints books challenge readers to question their own strongly held opinions and assumptions. Most people form their opinions on the basis of upbringing, peer pressure, and personal, cultural, or professional bias. By reading carefully balanced opposing views, readers must directly confront new ideas as well as the opinions of those with whom they disagree. This is not to simplistically argue that everyone who reads opposing views will—or should—change his or her opinion. Instead, the series enhances readers' understanding of their own views by encouraging confrontation with opposing ideas. Careful examination of others' views can lead to the readers' understanding of the logical inconsistencies in their own opinions, perspective on why they hold an opinion, and the consideration of the possibility that their opinion requires further evaluation.

Evaluating Other Opinions

To ensure that this type of examination occurs, Opposing Viewpoints books present all types of opinions. Prominent spokespeople on different sides of each issue as well as well-known professionals from many disciplines challenge the reader. An additional goal of the series is to provide a forum for other, less known, or even unpopular viewpoints. The opinion of an ordinary person who has had to make the decision to cut off life support from a terminally ill relative, for example, may be just as valuable and provide just as much insight as a medical ethicist's professional opinion. The editors have two additional purposes in including these less known views. One, the editors encourage readers to respect others' opinions—even when not enhanced by professional credibility. It is only by reading or listening to and objectively evaluating others' ideas that one can determine whether they are worthy of consideration. Two, the inclusion of such viewpoints encourages the important critical thinking skill of objectively evaluating an author's credentials and bias. This evaluation will illuminate an author's reasons for taking a particular stance on an issue and will aid in readers' evaluation of the author's ideas.

It is our hope that these books will give readers a deeper understanding of the issues debated and an appreciation of the complexity of even seemingly simple issues when good and honest people disagree. This awareness is particularly important in a democratic society such as ours in which people enter into public debate to determine the common good. Those with whom one disagrees should not be regarded as enemies but rather as people whose views deserve careful examination and may shed light on one's own.

Thomas Jefferson once said that "difference of opinion leads to inquiry, and inquiry to truth." Jefferson, a broadly educated man, argued that "if a nation expects to be ignorant and free . . . it expects what never was and never will be." As individuals and as a nation, it is imperative that we consider the opinions of others and examine them with skill and discernment. The Opposing Viewpoints Series is intended to help readers achieve this goal.

David L. Bender and Bruno Leone,
Founders

Introduction

"Public school advocates and critics often see the virtual monopoly of U.S. public education from opposite, if not opposing, sides, each fearing the other in interesting ways. Supporters of the public school system are worried that conservative politicians will continue to advocate for greater 'privatization' of public education, turning education into a more market-driven system. Such policies would undoubtedly allocate more public funds to private firms as well as to parents, who can choose a nonpublic education for their children, leading to the deflection of students and public tax funds away from public schools."

"Meanwhile, critics of public education— and supporters of more education choice—fear the incredible political power of the public school system, which is governed by local school boards, state legislatures and governors, and the federal government, all boosted by traditional public education interest groups like teachers' unions, school administrator associations, and liberal public interest lobbies."

Bruce S. Cooper and E. Vance Randall, Educational Policy, January 2008.

In a January 2008 issue of *Education Week*, Denis P. Doyle notes one way in which higher education differs from elementary and secondary public education. Quoting Harvard University President Derek Bok, Doyle states that higher education is more economically robust than its counterpart because colleges and universities come in two- and four-year varieties, are supported by for-profit and nonprofit providers, and offer many options to cater to students' schedules and needs. In short, higher education is a market driven by supply and demand. On the other hand, Doyle paints grade schools as "protected monopolies" run by regulations, not market forces. In this controlled environment, schools are not rewarded for innovation and therefore have no incentive to progress. Doyle adds, "Not only are there no incentives or rewards to change, there is active hostility to change."

Like other advocates of market-based schools, Doyle envisions facilities catering to the skills of the students, building class schedules around the times they can afford to be in school, and rewarding teachers for accomplishments, not merely time served. Doyle's dream, however, is not new. In 1992 Edison Schools Incorporated began the for-profit co-managing of elementary schools in America and Britain. Edison claimed it could run school districts for less money than traditional school boards had and raise students' performance. The company began trading its shares in the public market, but by 2001 it reported only one profitable quarter. In 2002 Edison was in financial trouble, and in the following year, it turned private after being bailed out by a pension firm in Florida. Edison never completely ran a private school—as it hoped to do; instead it continues to partner with some school districts in nineteen states, providing mainly curriculum assistance and professional development services. Edison claims that it has improved academic achievement in some of its partner facilities, but critics dispute these assertions.

In a 2003 article for the *Washington Post*, Janice Solkov, a former principal of an Edison school in Philadelphia, wrote an indictment of the Edison program as she experienced it.

Solkov describes how the per-student budget was set so low that promised computers were not made available for students, foreign language classes had to be cut, and key support staff had to be let go. When a sixth-grade teacher resigned unexpectedly, Solkov could not get Edison to find or fund a replacement. Eventually, Solkov resigned her position but conceded that Edison might have had better hopes of succeeding if its administrators had afforded more preparatory time and had the financial backing to make good on its promises. "The children, of course, are the ones who get lost in the endless shuffle of well-intentioned but mismanaged reform movements," Solkov concludes, though she maintains that private corporations need to bow out gracefully if they run into the kinds of trouble encountered in Philadelphia.

Proponents of privatization contend that the children are benefiting from these programs. Although many agree that test scores may not differ between privatized and public schools, advocates suggest that other factors may be just as important to students and parents when it comes to judging improvement. For example, the greater feeling of safety in privatized schools or the newfound access to better tools (computers, lab equipment, etc.) may influence students and parents to choose privatized schools. Defenders of privatization also argue that charter schools (schools that are granted charters to operate under private management) and vouchers (certificates that allow low-income parents to send their children to private schools) tend to create a mix of students, which helps end racial and economic segregation common among private and public institutions in poorer neighborhoods.

The reality of segregation, however, may not be so easily overcome. In fact, critics of charter schools, for example, insist that these institutions widen racial and economic divides. The *Boston Globe* reported that Boston's pilot charter schools "demand[ed] student transcripts, teacher recommendations, and essays from applicants" wishing to enroll. They also required parents to contribute forty hours per week of volunteer service in the district. In this way, charter schools can cherry-pick students who are most likely to succeed academically and thus improve the school's performance record. Other students, who may be more academically challenged (and in need of assistance) are supposedly left behind in the failing schools.

While such concerns are prevalent in the privatization debate, part of critics' distaste with privatization is the belief that education is not something that should be bought and sold in a marketplace. As social critic Noam Chomsky writes, "A public education system is based on the principle that you care whether the kid down the street gets an education." Chomsky argues that corporatization has no compassion; its sole function is to maximize profits. "You don't expect corporations to be benevolent any more than you expect dictatorships to be benevolent. . . . And one of the effects . . . is the undermining of the conception of solidarity and cooperation"—values that Chomsky associates with democracy and a compassionate society.

Mark Harrison, one of the authors in the following anthology, would not take issue with Chomsky's pro-democracy claims if idealism ruled school boards. As Harrison contends, "In the current system, decisions about public provision of education are made through the political process. This does not automatically result in policies that are in the best interest of children. . . . Political control of schools may be used to benefit politically powerful special-interest groups rather than please consumers, promote the public interest, or help the disadvantaged." He believes that providing services that students and parents prize and are willing to pay for will shape schools for the better. And this is why he favors privatized, market-driven education.

Harrison is but one author in *Opposing Viewpoints: Education*, which offers views on how education in America should or should not be altered. In chapters titled "What Is the State of Education in America?" "Are Alternatives to Public Education Viable?" "Should Religious and Moral Values Be Taught as Part of Public Education?" and "How Should the Education System Be Improved?" these authors dissect the current educational system and propose remedial or revolutionary policies to improve outcomes for both students and teachers. Privatization—and its related concerns such as school vouchers and charter programs—remains a prominent topic that clearly divides proponents and critics into their respective camps. So, too, do issues such as the separation of church and state and the lingering effects of segregation half a century after the mandated integration of the public school system. All of these topics force students, parents, teachers, administrators, and government officials to continually reexamine the state of education in the United States to see if it is living up to its promise of preparing the next generation for the world that lies ahead.

CHAPTER 1

What Is the State of Education in America?

Chapter Preface

In December 2007 the Program for International Student Assessment (PISA) published the results of its most recent (2006) statistical surveys of mathematics and science literacy among fifteen-year-olds in fifty-seven nations, including the United States. In science, American students ranked below the international average, with nearly a quarter failing to demonstrate minimal scientific literacy. Even America's top-scoring students were outperformed by higher-achieving peers in twelve other nations. The United States fared similarly in mathematics. American students fell below the average, and those of the highest rank were still outperformed by their foreign counterparts in twenty-nine other countries.

Many commentators interpret these "below-average" rankings as a sign of America's unpreparedness for a global future dominated by science and technology. Writing of the 2003 PISA test, in which the United States made a similar showing, June Krunholz claimed that poor math scores reveal "the U.S. lacks the advantage of a generally well-educated population" necessary to ensure economic growth in a globalizing marketplace. Others have called attention to the fact that while America's performance has not improved statistically from the first PISA test in 2000, other nations have seen rising test scores over the years, suggesting their understanding that future prosperity will rely on expertise in these areas of knowledge.

The concern that America is forsaking its future, however, is not shared by all reviewers of the PISA statistics. Writing in Utah's *Deseret News*, Walt Gardner argues that the tests do not take into account the diverse population of the United States in comparison to leading PISA test-scoring nations such as Japan, Germany, and Italy. Gardner writes:

America's diverse student population and disparate social conditions . . . are given short shrift. Germany's and Italy's students are nearly 100 percent white; Japan's are nearly 100 percent Asian.

Ninety-nine percent of Japan's population speaks Japanese as their first language. On the flip side, 18 percent of the U.S. population lives in a household where a language other than English is spoken. Single-parent households with children under age 17 account for 33 percent of families in America, compared with less than 10 percent in Japan, Singapore and Korea.

Yet whether the socioeconomic disparities or the growing immigrant population are distorting America's results is still a subject of debate. Gardner contends that tests are poor indicators of future preparedness. He cites critics from the 1980s who predicted America would collapse due to its supposedly failing school system. Noting that America still holds incredible technical capital in the early twenty-first century, he dismisses such worries as baseless. In the following chapter, commentators and critics argue other aspects of the state of education in America. Some continue to warn of coming disaster, while others insist that the nation's schools are still fighting to ensure that all Americans receive a fair and useful education.

| "The fact is, the restructured education
system has been designed to deliberately dumb-down the children."

Public Education Is Failing

Tom DeWeese

*In the following viewpoint, Tom DeWeese argues that the Ameri-
can education system is failing to adequately educate students in
traditional academic subjects such as reading, writing, and mathematics. DeWeese maintains that students are instead subjected
to an education system concerned only with promoting the political and economic agenda of liberal politicians and teachers'
unions. With all recent reforms failing to address the root of the
problem—the bureaucratic Department of Education—the author states that education will continue to decline until a leader
decides to tackle the problem. Tom DeWeese is the president of
the American Policy Center, a public-policy organization advo-
cating free enterprise and limited government regulation in
American business and life.*

As you read, consider the following questions:

1. According to DeWeese, what are the two educational
   categories in which the United States leads the rest of
   the world?

Tom DeWeese, "American Education Fails Because It Isn't Education," NewsWith
Views.com, December 10, 2007, www.newswithviews.com/DeWeese/tom99.htm. Reproduced by permission.

2. What entities does DeWeese claim have benefited from the restructuring of the education system?

3. According to the work of Charlotte Iserbyt mentioned by DeWeese, how and for what purpose did the "education establishment" pursue the restructuring of the U.S. education system?

The debate over public education grows more heated. Regularly, reports are released showing that the academic abilities of American students continue to fall when compared to those in other countries.

Twenty years ago the U.S. ranked first in the world in the number of young adults who had high school diplomas and college degrees. Today we rank ninth and seventh, respectively, among industrialized nations. Compared to Europe and Asia, 15-year-olds in the United States are below average in applying math skills to real-life tasks. The United States ranks 18 out of 24 industrialized nations in terms of relative effectiveness of its education system. Knowledge in history, geography, grammar, civics and literature are all in decline in terms of academic understanding and achievement.

To solve the crisis, politicians, community leaders and the education community all preach the same mantra. Students fail, they tell us, because "expectations haven't been set high enough." We need more "accountability," they say. And every education leader and nearly every politician presents the same "solution" to the education crisis: more money, better pay for teachers, and smaller classroom numbers so the children get enough attention from the teachers.

Excelling in the Wrong Categories

Consequently, there are two specific categories in which the U.S. excels, compared to the rest of the world. First, the U.S. ranks second in the world in the amount we spend per student per year on education = $11,152. The U.S. is also a leader in having some of the smallest classroom numbers in the world. Yet the slide continues. American students grow more illiterate by the year. How can that be? We're doing everything the "experts" tell us to do. We're spending the money. We're building more and more schools. We're raising teachers' pay.

Every American should understand that these three items: higher pay, smaller classrooms and more money for schools are the specific agenda of the National Education Association (NEA). The NEA is not a professional organization for teachers. It is a labor union and its sole job is to get more money into the education system, and more pay for its members. It also seeks to make work easier for its members—smaller classrooms. Clearly the NEA is not about education—it's about money and a political agenda.

Clearly the nation's education system is not teaching the children. They can't read or work math problems without a calculator. They can't spell, find their own country on a map, name the president of the United States or quote a single Founding Father. America's children are becoming just plain dumb.

Ignoring the Root of the Problem

Yet we have been focusing on a massive national campaign to "fix" the schools for the past decade or more. Now we have ultra high-tech, carpeted, air-conditioned school buildings with computers and television sets. We have education programs full of new ideas, new methods, and new directions. In the 1990s we set "national standards," accountability through "national testing" through Goals 2000. Through that program we declared that every child would come to school "ready to learn," "no child would be left behind," and pledged that our kids would be "second to none" in the world. Above all, we've spent money, money and more money. The result, American students have fallen further behind, placing 19th out of 21 nations in math, 16th in science and dead last in physics.

With all the programs and attention on education, how can that be? To coin a well-worn cliché—"it's the programs, stupid." More precisely, it's the federal programs and the education bureaucracy that run them. It is simply a fact that over the past twenty years America's education system has been completely restructured to deliberately move away from teaching basic academics to a system that focuses on little more than training students for menial jobs. The fact is, the restructured education system has been designed to deliberately dumb-down the children. (Note: the NEA hates that phrase!)

Most Americans find that statement to be astonishing and, in fact, to be beyond belief. Parents don't want to let go of their child-like faith that the American education system is the best in the world, designed to give their children the academic strength to make them the smartest in the world. Politicians continue to offer old solutions of more money and more federal attention, almost stamping their feet, demanding that kids learn something. Programs are being proposed that call for teacher testing to hold them accountable for producing educated children. More programs call for annual tests to find out if children have learned anything. The nation is in panic. But none of these hysterical responses will improve education—because none of them address the very root of the problem.

The truth is, none of the problems will go away, nor will children learn until both parents and politicians stop trusting the education establishment and start ridding the system of its failed ideas and programs. Parents and politicians must stop believing the propaganda handed down by the education establishment that says teaching a child in the twenty-first century is different and must be more high tech than in days past. It simply isn't so.

Benefiting Everyone Except Students

Today's education system is driven by money from the federal government and private foundations, both working hand-in-hand with the education establishment headquartered in the federal Department of Education and manned by the National Education Association (NEA). These forces have combined with psychologists, huge textbook publishers, teacher colleges, the health care profession, government bureaucrats, big corporations, pharmaceutical companies and social workers to invade local school boards, classrooms and private homes in the name of "fixing" education.

The record shows that each of these entities has benefited from this alliance through enriched coffers and increased political power. In fact, the new education restructuring is working wonders for everyone involved—except for the children and their parents. As a result of this combined invasion force, today's classroom is a very different place from only a few years ago.

There is simply not enough room on these pages to tell the entire history of education restructuring and transformation. It dates back to the early efforts by psychologists like John Dewey, whose work began to change how teachers were taught to teach in the nation's teacher colleges. The changes were drastic as education moved away from an age-old system that taught teachers how to motivate students to accept the whole scope of academic information available. Instead the new system explored methods to maneuver students through psychological behavior modification processes. Rather than to instill knowledge, once such a power was established the education process became more of a method to instill specific agendas into the minds of children.

Restructuring Education Toward the Psychological

As fantastic as it seems, the entire history of the education restructuring effort is carefully and thoroughly documented in a book called *The Deliberate Dumbing Down of America*. The book was written by Charlotte Thomson Iserbyt, a former of-

"Can We 'Dumb It Down' a Bit, Mrs. Whipplemore?" Cartoon by Dan Rosandich. CartoonStock.com.

ficial at the Department of Education in the [Ronald] Reagan Administration. While there in 1981–1982, Charlotte found the "mother lode" hidden away at the Department. In short, she found all of the education establishment's plans for restructuring America's classrooms. Not only did she find the plans for what they intended to do, she discovered how they were going to do it and most importantly why. Since uncovering this monstrous plan, Charlotte Iserbyt has dedicated her life to getting that information into the hands of parents, politicians and the news media

Iserbyt's work details how the process to restructure America's education system began at the beginning of the twentieth century and slowly picked up speed over the decades. The new system used psychology-based curriculum to slowly change the attitudes, values and beliefs of the students.

The new school agenda was very different from most people's understanding of the purpose of American education. NEA leader William Carr, secretary of the Educational Policies Commission, clearly stated that new agenda when in 1947 he wrote in the *NEA Journal*: "The teaching profession prepares the leaders of the future. . . . The statesmen, the industrialists, the lawyers, the newspapermen . . . all the leaders of tomorrow are in schools today." Carr went on to write: "The psychological foundations for wider loyalties must be laid. . . . Teach those attitudes which will result ultimately in the creation of a world citizenship and world government . . . we can and should teach those skills and attitudes which will help to create a society in which world citizenship is possible."

Professor Benjamin Bloom, called the Father of Outcome-Based Education (OBE) said: "The purpose of education and the schools is to change the thoughts, feelings and actions of students." B.F. Skinner determined that applied psychology in the class curriculum was the means to bring about such changes in the students values and beliefs simply by relentlessly inputting specific programmed messages. Skinner once bragged: "I could make a pigeon a high achiever by reinforcing it on a proper schedule." Whole psychological studies were produced to prove that individuals could be made to believe anything, even to accept that black was white, given the proper programming.

Deliberately De-Emphasizing Education

The education system is now a captive of the Skinner model of behavior modification programming. In 1990, Dr. M. Donald Thomas perfectly outlined the new education system in an article in *The Effective School Report* entitled "Education 90: A Framework for the Future." Thomas said:

From Washington to modern times, literacy has meant the ability to read and write, the ability to understand numbers, and the capacity to appreciate factual material. The world, however, has changed dramatically in the last 30 years. The introduction of technology in information processing, the compression of the world into a single economic system, and the revolution in political organizations are influences never imagined to be possible in our lifetime. . . . Literacy, therefore, will be different in the year 2000. It will mean that students will need to follow.

- Appreciation of different cultures, differences in belief systems and differences in political structures

- An understanding of communications and the ability of people to live in one world as one community of nations . . .

- In a compressed world with one economic system . . . it is especially important that all our people be more highly educated and that the differences between low and high socioeconomic students be significantly narrowed . . .

- Education begins at birth and ends at death . . .

- Education is a responsibility to be assumed by the whole community . . .

- Learning how to learn is more important than memorizing facts

- Schools form partnerships with community agencies for public service projects to be a part of schooling . . .

Rewards are provided for encouraging young people to perform community service.

In this one outline, Dr. Thomas provides the blueprint for today's education system that is designed to de-emphasize academic knowledge; establish the one-world agenda with the

United Nations as its center and away from belief in national sovereignty; replace individual achievement with collectivist group-think ideology and invade the family with an "It takes a village" mind-set. Dr. Thomas's outline for education is the root of why today's children aren't learning. These ideas permeate every federal program, every national standard, every textbook and every moment of your child's school day.

Recent Plans for Reform

Upon election, President [George W.] Bush declared education to be his number one priority. His first legislation to reach the hill was a major education policy proposal called: "No Child Left Behind." The president said education was the hallmark of his time as Governor of Texas where he imposed strict guidelines for annual testing. He says he wanted to confront the growing problem of American illiteracy and the low standing of test scores. And the president said, "We must focus the spending of federal tax dollars on things that work."

To those ends, the President's education policy proposal addresses four specific principles including: 1) Annual testing to assure the schools are actually teaching the children and achieving specific educational goals. 2) Restore local control by giving local and state school boards the "flexibility to innovate." Said the President, "educational entrepreneurs should not be hindered by excessive red tape and regulation." 3) Stop funding failure. The President proposed several options for helping failing schools to improve. 4) Give parents a choice to find a school that does teach. President Bush gave schools a specific period of time to improve. If they failed, parents would be given the option of going to another, more successful school by way of a voucher plan.

On the surface these proposals sounded to many like fresh new ideas to take back local control of the schools and run the federal programs out the door. But time and a closer examination proved otherwise. In fact, President Bush himself unknowingly summed up the problem with his education program with one statement: "Change will not come by disdaining or dismantling the federal role of education."

Continued Ignorance of the Real Problem

To the great disappointment of many, President Bush decided to completely ignore the very root of the education problem—the federal government and its programs. Instead, President Bush's proposal accepted the incorrect conclusion that the problem with education is simply an over blown bureaucracy that wastes federal funds and fails to enforce clear standards by rewarding bad schools. His numerous statements that "no child will be left behind," came straight from the decade-old motto of the Children's Defense Fund, the group that claims Hillary Clinton as one of its leaders. By being so off-the-mark, there just is no way the Bush proposal could appropriately address a single school reform issue.

First, his plan to restore local control was directly tied to the use of Title I federal funding. Title I is one of the main federal programs to directly fund the "at-risk" catch-all device now driving the invasion of in-home social workers; the establishment of in-school health clinics; the enforcement of pop diagnosis by teachers and administrators that has put millions of children on Ritalin. Title I is the root of the education establishment's attack on families.

Second, by leaving the federal Department of Education intact, President Bush left in full force the machinery now driving the education system. State school boards are simply outposts of the federal bureaucrats. They are of the same mind-set, driving the same programs in the states that are dictated by the federal office. Local ideas from local teachers and parents have no chance of a hearing in these vast bureaucracies. Failing to address this behemoth simply dooms any attempt to improve education. . . .

The Bush plan ignored the existence of the social scientists who have made psychological guinea pigs out of the children. It ignored the role of the Department of Education as a teacher training lab which brags that, in just two weeks, it can completely change the attitudes, values and beliefs of good, academically-focused teachers, and turn them into pliable facilitators to help dumb-down the very students they sought to teach. Nothing was changed in the classroom under the Bush plan.

Time for New Education Reform Policies

From the start of his administration, President Bush made it clear that he had no intention of getting rid of the Department of Education. Consequently, the Republican dominated Congress dropped its intentions to de-fund and remove the Department of Education. However, it is not possible to make the changes that Americans are hoping for without taking that step. Bush's plan simply used warm and fuzzy rhetoric to further institutionalize more of the same. His voucher plan has proven to be little more than a Judas Goat to lead private schools into the nightmare of federal programs, which attack and feed on any school that accepts federal money. And so the cancer grows.

While promising to fix American education, the President doomed any hope of it by insisting on keeping the establishment intact. The "No Child Left Behind" Act simply succeeded in institutionalizing the failed policies of Goals 2000 and School to Work. And that's why American education continues to fall.

It's time to ignore the agenda of a self-interested labor union and begin to look at the real reasons why American public schools are in crisis. What is robbing our children of the ability to get a good education?

Americans who want to rid the nation of this plague have little choice but to insist that their representatives in Congress begin a complete investigation into the Department of Education and its policies, its waste and its fraud on the taxpayers, parents and children of this nation.

Perhaps then, as the facts are exposed under the hot lights of a congressional hearing, the American people will begin to understand that the problem with education isn't low-paid teachers and crowded classrooms—but rather, is the result of a cynical, deliberate attempt to dumb-down America to promote a radical political agenda. For that is the truth.

> "In the midst of the culture wars that
> swirl around schools . . . it is easy to
> lose sight of the broader purpose and
> grand vision of the common public
> school."

Public Education
Is Not Failing

Mike Rose

*Mike Rose contends in the following viewpoint that the ongoing
debate about the failures of public schools obscures the value and
daily achievement of the public school system. While conceding
that public schools can and should always be improved, Rose
goes on to state that the current language used to describe public
schools is not helpful in finding ways to address problems within
the U.S. education system. Further, he argues that the general
discontent with public schools is not reflective of the state of education, but rather is part of a larger disillusionment with and
distrust of all public entities. Mike Rose, a professor of education
at the University of California, Los Angeles, authored the books*
Possible Lives: The Promise of Public Education in America

Mike Rose, "Grand Visions and Possible Lives," as first appeared in *Education Week*,
October 11, 2006. Copyright © 2006 Editorial Projects in Education. Reprinted with
permission from the author.

and Lives on the Boundary: A Moving Account of the Struggles and Achievements of America's Educationally Underprepared.

As you read, consider the following questions:

1. What two ways of talking about public schools does the author say constrain how the problems of public schools are framed?
2. How do U.S. citizens currently view the idea of "the public," according to Rose?
3. What instances does Rose say reminded him of what is possible in America's public sphere?

"We can all agree," wrote a contributing editor for *The Weekly Standard* not long ago, "that American public schools are a joke." This way of thinking and talking about our public schools has been with us for some time. It was what led me, in the early and mid-1990s, on a cross-country journey to observe a wide variety of public schools that had been judged by their teachers, students, and parents to be good and decent places of learning. This journey was both geographical—recording actual classrooms and communities across the United States—and philosophical, trying to gain a lived, felt sense of what public education means in a democracy. The result was a book called *Possible Lives*. Now, a decade after its publication, the same kind of reflective journey is more needed than ever.

The Daily Details of Public Education

In the midst of the culture wars that swirl around schools; the fractious, intractable school politics; the conservative assault on public institutions; and the testing, testing, testing—in the midst of all this, it is easy to lose sight of the broader purpose and grand vision of the common public school. For me, that grand vision came through, fresh and vibrant, in the common, everyday detail of classrooms, the words and gestures of a good teacher, the looks on the faces of students thinking their way through a problem.

We have so little of such detail in our national discussion of teaching, learning, or the very notion of public education itself. It has all become a contentious abstraction. But detail gives us the sense of a place, something that can get lost in policy discussions about our schools—or, for that matter, in so much of our national discussion about ourselves. Too often, we deal in broad brush strokes about regions, about politics and economics, about racial, linguistic, and other social characteristics. Witness the red state-blue state distinction [between states which generally vote conservative and liberal respectively], one that, yes, tells us something quick and consequential about averages, but misses so much about local social and political dynamics, the lived civic variability within.

The details of classroom life convey, in a specific and physical way, the intellectual work being done, day to day, across the nation—the feel and clatter of teaching and learning. I'm thinking right now of a moment from a chemistry class in Pasadena, Calif., that I observed. The students had been conducting experiments to determine the polarity of various materials. Some were washing test tubes, holding them up to the windows for the glint of sunlight, checking for a bad rinse. Some were mixing salt and water to prepare one of their polar materials. Some were cautiously filling droppers with hydrochloric acid or carbon tetrachloride. And some were stirring solutions with glass rods, squinting to see the results. There was lots of chatter and lots of questions of the teacher, who walked from student to student, asking what they were doing and why, and what they were finding out.

The students were learning about the important concept of polarity. They were also learning to be systematic and methodical. And moving through the room was the teacher, asking questions, responding, fostering a scientific cast of mind.

Reframing the Debate on How to Improve Education

This sort of classroom scene is not rare. And collectively, such moments give a palpable sense of what it means to have, distributed across a nation, available by law to all, a public educational system to provide the opportunity for such intellectual development.

Without a doubt, there is much that is wrong with our schools. Citizens in a democracy must continually assess the performance of their public institutions. But the quality and language of that evaluation matter. Before we can evaluate, we need to be clear about what it is we're evaluating, what the nature of the thing is: its variables and intricacies, its goals and purpose. We should also ask why we're evaluating. To what end?

Neither the sweeping rhetoric of public school failure nor the continual focus on test scores helps us here. Both exclude the important, challenging work done daily in schools across the country, thereby limiting the educational vocabulary and imagery available to us. This way of talking about schools constrains the way we frame problems and blinkers our imagination.

A Broad Disillusionment with All Things Public

There have been times in our history when the idea of "the public" has been invested with great agency and imagination. Such is not the case now. An entire generation has come of age amid disillusionment with public institutions and public life, disillusionment born of high-profile government scandal and institutional inefficiency, but, more so, from a skillful advocacy by conservative policymakers and pundits of the broad virtues of free markets and individual enterprise.

Clearly, there are domains of public life that benefit from market forces, and individual enterprise is a powerful force for

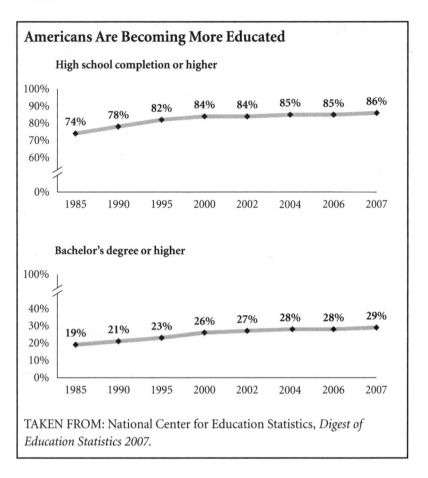

Americans Are Becoming More Educated

High school completion or higher

100%
90%   82%   84%   84%   85%   85%   86%
80%   74%   78%
70%
60%

0%
     1985   1990   1995   2000   2002   2004   2006   2007

Bachelor's degree or higher

100%

40%
30%   23%   26%   27%   28%   28%   29%
20%   19%   21%
10%
0%
     1985   1990   1995   2000   2002   2004   2006   2007

TAKEN FROM: National Center for Education Statistics, *Digest of Education Statistics 2007*.

both personal advancement and public benefit. Moreover, the very notion of "public" is a fluid one; it changes historically, exists in varied relationships to the private sector, and, on occasion, fuses with that sector in creative ways. And, as I have noted, we must not simply accept our public institutions as they are, but be vigilantly engaged with them.

Our reigning orthodoxy on the public sphere is much less nuanced. Instead, we celebrate the market and private initiative as cure-alls to our social and civic obligations.

This easy dismissiveness of the public sector also has its ugly side, characterizing anything public as inferior . . . or worse. I remember a Los Angeles talk-show host who called the children enrolled in the Los Angeles school district "garbage." And, in a comment both telling and sad, the kids I met during my travels said on several occasions that they knew people thought of them as "debris."

Revitalizing the Notion of Public Schools

We have to do better than this. We have to develop a revitalized sense of public life and public education.

One tangible resource for such a revitalization became clear to me over the course of my journey through America's public school classrooms. Out of the thousands of small, daily events of classroom life I witnessed—out of the details of the work done there—I gained a deeper appreciation for what's possible in America's public sphere.

This sense of the possible came to me when a child learned to take another child seriously, to think something through with other children, to learn about perspective and the range of human experience and talent. It came when, over time, a child arrived at an understanding of number, or acquired skill in rendering an idea in written language. It came when a group of students crowded around a lab table trying to figure out why a predicted reaction fizzled. When a local event or regional dialect or familiar tall tale became a creative resource for visual art or spoken word. When a developing athlete planted the pole squarely in the box and vaulted skyward. When a student said that his teacher "coaxes our thinking along." When a teacher, thinking back on it all, mused on the power of "watching your students at such an important time in their lives encounter the world."

There is, of course, nothing inherently public or private about such activities. They occur daily in private schools, in church organizations, in backyards. But there is something compelling, I think, about raising one's gaze outward, beyond the immediate window or fence, to the science lesson at the forest's edge or the novel crammed into the hip pocket on the city bus.

The public school gives rise to these moments in a common space, supports them, commits to them as a public good, affirms the capacity of all of us, contributes to what the post-Revolutionary War writer Samuel Harrison Smith called the "general diffusion of knowledge" across the republic. Such a mass public endeavor creates a citizenry.

As our notion of the public shrinks, the full meaning of public education, the cognitive and social luxuriance of it, fades. Achievement is still possible, but it loses its civic heart.

> *"Standardized tests are now used to hold up children and schools for comparison; the scores are used to discriminate rather than diagnose, punish rather than reward."*

Standardized Testing Has Negatively Impacted Public Schools

Bobbie A. Solley

The emphasis placed on standardized testing has had a significant negative impact on the public education system in the United States, according to Bobbie A. Solley in the following viewpoint. Solley argues that schools no longer strive to create informed citizens; instead, they focus only on teaching children what is essential for them to know to pass the government-mandated standardized tests. As a result, children's motivation and learning as well as classroom curriculum suffer, Solley claims. Bobbie A. Solley is a professor of elementary and special education at Middle Tennessee State University.

Bobbie A. Solley, "On Standardized Testing: An ACEI Position Paper," *Childhood Education*, Fall 2007, pp. 31–37. Copyright © 2007 by the Association. Reproduced by permission of the Association for Childhood Education International, 17904 Georgia Avenue, Suite 215, Olney, MD.

As you read, consider the following questions:

1. From the time it was developed until the early part of the twentieth century, what was the purpose of public education in the United States, according to Solley?

2. As Solley claims, on what were standardized education tests developed after World War I based?

3. What are the three areas of education that the author asserts are negatively effected by standardized testing?

Following the whirlwind standards movement of the 1980s, the beginning of the 1990s ushered in an overwhelming interest in and use of testing to document students' progress. In 1991, the Association for Childhood Education International (ACEI) [an international organization dedicated to improving education for children worldwide] issued its second position paper calling for a moratorium on standardized testing in the early years of schooling (the first one on that topic was published in 1976) (ACEI/Perrone, 1991). Citing the rising use of tests to label children, place children in special programs, and retain underachieving children in a grade level, ACEI denounced the use of these tests in the early grades and questioned their use in later grades as well. It was the hope that more discussions would ensue concerning the negative effects of standardized testing on children's learning and their motivation to learn. The Association leadership further hoped that schools would more actively pursue assessment alternatives that honored children's individuality and developmental growth.

While discussion has certainly increased in both content and intensity and alternatives have been explored, we have not seen a significant change in the use (and, in many cases, the misuse) of testing. With the advent of the No Child Left Behind law [legislation to reform the U.S. education system], enacted in 2002, quality developmentally appropriate teaching and learning practices have taken a backseat to the more focused attention on low-level skills that can be assessed easily on a standardized multiple-choice test. Standardized tests are now used to hold up children and schools for comparison; the scores are used to discriminate rather than diagnose, punish rather than reward. Equally disturbing is the misuse of these tests—and these tests alone—to unjustly hold teachers and schools accountable and then punish those who have not met adequate yearly progress, as deemed by people other than those working with children on a daily basis (e.g., politicians).

When Vito Perrone [then professor at the Harvard Graduate School of Education] updated ACEI's position paper on testing in 1991, he claimed that a testing moratorium was even more important than it had been in 1976; I believe the need has continued to grow. Excellent teachers are leaving the profession out of frustration. High-quality schools that serve children from disenfranchised homes are being closed and children displaced. Important skills that schools once taught, such as critical thinking, discussions, and problem solving, are being replaced by low-level, fill-in-the-blank worksheets and drills. The gap between the poor and the rich is ever-widening, and there appears to be no end in sight. It is past time for teachers, schools, administrators, parents, and the public to stand up and let their voices be heard. It is past time for all involved to put a stop to the *misuse* of tests in all grades, particularly in the primary years.

Public Schools Highlight Differences

The United States is a nation built on the ideals of freedom and equality, a nation of principles and responsibilities. It is a nation of wealth and power, a land of opportunity where democratic values are honored and people strive to help children succeed. At the same time, it is a nation of the poor and indigent, a land where families are impoverished and disempowered. For those children who come from homes that struggle under the burden of financial stress and poverty, the fruits of democracy can appear out of reach.

For many children, U.S. public schools have become places where separateness is evident, where those who do not have are expected to achieve the same standards as those who have. School, the very place where democratic values should be taught and practiced, is being eroded in the name of standardized testing and accountability. As a result, many voices have been silenced.

The Purpose of Public Education

[As W. James Popham wrote in his 2001 book, *The Truth About Testing*,] "Public education is the latchkey that can open the door to a land of opportunity; it is the cornerstone of our nation's democratic system of government." From the earliest days of the United States and into the early part of the 20th century, public education was revered and applauded for its success in educating children of all backgrounds. It was esteemed as the necessary tool for the country to continue thriving, as informed citizens are critical to a true democracy. . . .

Public school, by its very nature, was intended to secure for children their place in a democratic society with the knowledge, understanding, and tools necessary to make decisions for the good of all its citizens.

During the late 1960s and early 1970s, an increasing rumble of discontent concerning the nation's schools began. What are our schools doing? What are our schools teaching? What are our children learning? Where is our money going? Are our children being prepared to take their place in the competitive world here and abroad? With these questions came suspicion and then distrust in the nation's teachers and schools. In order to combat the mounting disregard for public education, the federal government took steps that would change the landscape of education in the United States and threaten the very fabric of democracy.

Tests to Discriminate Between Test-Takers

Were the mounting suspicions a result of failing schools? Or, were there other factors at work? Standardized achievement tests had their beginning not in public schools, but within a branch of the military during World War I. The war brought about a great need for officers. Consequently, army officials asked the American Psychological Association to develop a group-administered test that would help identify the recruits most likely to succeed in the Army's officer training program. Around that time, the use of the Stanford-Binet tests, which produced what became known as IQ scores, became widespread. In 1917, a committee convened and developed 10 different subtests that were designed to [in Popham's words] "discriminate among test-takers with respect to their intellectual abilities." These were known as the Army Alpha Tests and were given to a norm group that would be used as a comparison mark for more than a million men getting ready for combat. Those ranked high would be selected for officer training, while those ranked lower would be relegated to the battlefield. Within a short time following World War I, new educational tests were copyrighted that mimicked the Army Alpha in its measurement strategy.

Another factor contributing to the spread of standardized testing was the far-reaching Elementary and Secondary Education Act (ESEA). In 1965, President Lyndon Johnson, concerned with the growing numbers of children living in disadvantaged homes, issued ESEA as he launched his war on poverty. For the first time, large amounts of federal money were awarded to states in order to help them bolster children's learning. These funds were specifically designed to offer assistance to schools that served large numbers of socially disadvantaged children. An addendum to the ESEA, offered by Senator Robert Kennedy, required states that received federal funds to evaluate and report on the effectiveness of their programs, namely via standardized achievement tests. These tests were based on the Army Alpha to discriminate among test takers. The tests available at the time, however, included the Metropolitan Achievement Tests and the Comprehensive Tests of Basic Skills, and bore no direct relationship to the skills and knowledge being promoted by any particular ESEA program. And yet, the government spent thousands of dollars in encouraging their use. The notion that a standardized achievement test could evaluate the success of various school- and district-wide programs was quickly followed by the notion that the same standardized achievement test could be used to evaluate learning as well. Despite the lack of research to back up this assertion, testing became the means to measure children's learning.

Standardized Testing for Accountability

To further compound the misuse of standardized testing, *A Nation At Risk* (National Commission for Excellence in Education, 1983) was published in 1983. The report decried the condition of public schools in the United States:

> Our nation is at risk. Our once unchallenged preeminence in commerce, industry, science, and technological innovation is being overtaken by competitors throughout the world. . . . We report to the American people . . . the educational foundations of our society are presently being eroded by a *rising tide of mediocrity that threatens our very future as a nation and as a people* [italics are mine].

What Johnson's War on Poverty could not do with additional tests and accountability systems, *A Nation At Risk* would attempt to do. The report made recommendations in areas of content, standards, expectations, time, teaching, leadership, and fiscal support, and standardized tests became a pivotal part of evaluating the quality of education within each school in the country.

By the late 1980s, most states required some type of mandatory testing; by 1991, students who completed high school took, on average, 18–21 standardized tests in their career, with the majority of them occurring in the K–5 years. In 1994, President Clinton issued his landmark education package, Goals 2000: Educate America Act (P.L. 103-227). This act provided resources to states and communities to ensure that "all students reach their full potential." It established a framework by which to identify "world-class academic standards, to measure student progress, and provide the support that students may need to meet the standards." Central to this act was a National Standards Board and a call for voluntary testing in grades 4, 8, and 12 to ensure that standards were being met.

Recent Legislation Cements the Use of Testing

In 2002, the U.S. Congress signed into law President George W. Bush's No Child Left Behind (NCLB) initiative, which has been the most far-reaching education act since the War on Poverty in 1965 (No Child Left Behind Act, 2001). Testing children in 4th, 8th, and 12th grades is now mandatory. Accountability systems that require assessments to prove children's growth in academic subjects are mandatory. Tests are not simply what teachers give at the end of the year. They are now attached to high stakes, such as grade retention, admittance into special programs, graduation, admission into college, and whether or not schools remain open and teachers get to keep their jobs.

Today, because of NCLB, all 50 states have some form of standardized testing whereby students are tested every year, beginning in the 3rd grade. In many states, 1st- and 2nd-graders are also tested. And, in some states, kindergartners are tested regularly as well.

Large numbers of children are given standardized tests in two three-hour increments within a one- to two-week period each spring. The purpose of today's standardized achievement tests remains much the same as it was with the Army Alpha

(Popham, 2001). The test-takers' scores are compared to a pre-determined norm group to discriminate among them and determine rank. Today, it continues to be the mission of a standardized test-maker to develop a set of items that allows for making accurate comparisons among test-takers and then rank-ordering those who take the test. Standardized testing, as it gets more all-encompassing, has become a nightmare of huge proportion in the United States. As [education author and speaker] Alfie Kohn states, "Standardized testing has swelled and mutated, like a creature in one of those old horror movies, to the point that it now threatens to swallow our schools whole."

Although standardized tests historically have been loosely tied to accountability and student learning, the link has been tenuous. With the advent of No Child Left Behind, however, the connection between student learning and high-stakes standardized testing is more pronounced, and an increase in use of the tests has reached epic proportions. The premise behind this link is that increased pressure to do well on standardized tests, along with a set of rewards and punishments, will increase student learning and achievement. Does this actually occur, however? Are students learning more in our schools today? Are they more motivated to learn today than they were 40 years ago? Are more students staying in school and pursuing higher learning? The effects of testing have far-reaching consequences, not only on today's children but also on future generations of children. . . .

Testing Decreases Motivation

The assumption surrounding current testing methods is that children will be motivated to learn when the associated rewards and consequences are made clear. Yet, researchers have consistently found that an approach based on extrinsic rewards and consequences actually *reduces* children's intrinsic motivation to learn. . . . Because of high-stakes testing and the pressure that surrounds it, children are no longer engaged in enriching experiences for the pure joy of learning—experiences whereby they make decisions, explore options, make hypotheses, or problem solve. Extrinsic motivation, in the form of rewards and consequences, has replaced learning for the sheer pleasure of learning and the internal satisfaction that comes from a job well done. Children are now under increased pressure to perform on demand, memorize mundane facts and figures, and sit for long periods of time while listening to the teacher and/or filling in circles on a worksheet.

Research by [psychiatrist William] Glasser and [Carleen] Glasser (2003) indicates that stress increases the rate of aging and reduces the functioning of the immune system. The researchers also state that the worst kind of stress is caused when we have little or no control over our lives. As children are inundated with standardized tests, the resulting mundane methodologies of teaching in order to prepare for the test has both teachers and children feeling helpless. [Author and social critic Peter] Sacks (1999) also talks of the dangers of test-driven classrooms: "Test-driven classrooms exacerbate boredom, fear, lethargy, promoting all manner of mechanical behaviors on the part of teachers, students, and schools, and bleed school children of their natural love of learning."

Furthermore, an overreliance on extrinsic rewards and the subsequent lack of learning that follows has led to an increase in retention rates and an associated higher dropout rate. In Louisiana alone, between 10 and 15 percent of 4th- and 8th-graders were retained in 2000 because of failure to pass the state's high-stakes test. And, in Florida, in the spring of 2003, more than 43,000 third-graders (25 percent of the total for that grade level) were not allowed to advance to 4th grade, due to their insufficient scores on standardized tests. Because of the correlation between retention and dropout, motivation to learn and the desire to finish school has lessened. A study conducted by [researchers Sharon L.] Nichols, [Gene V.] Glass,

Making History Testable or Not Teaching It

[Since 2003], hundreds of schools, districts, states, and even the federal government have enacted policies that seek to restrict critical analysis of historical and contemporary events in the school curriculum. In June 2006, the Florida Education Omnibus Bill included language specifying that, "The history of the United States shall be taught as genuine history. . . . American history shall be viewed as factual, not as constructed, shall be viewed as knowable, teachable, and testable. . . ."

I focus on history teaching here, but the trend is not limited to social studies. In many states, virtually every subject area is under scrutiny for any deviation from one single narrative, based on knowable, testable, and purportedly uncontested facts. An English teacher, in a recent study undertaken by colleagues and myself, told us that even novel reading was now prescriptive in her state's rubric: meanings predetermined, vocabulary words pre-selected, and essay topics predigested. A science teacher put it this way: "The only part of the science curriculum now being critically analyzed is evolution."

As many people have observed, the high stakes testing mandated by No Child Left Behind (NCLB) has further pushed to the margins education efforts that challenge students to grapple with tough questions about society and the world. In a recent study by the Center on Education Policy, 71 percent of districts reported cutting back time for other subjects—social studies in particular—to make more space for reading and math instruction. . . .

Joel Westheimer, "No Child Left Thinking,"
Independent School, *Spring 2008.*

and [David C.] Berliner (2005) found that high-stakes testing pressure is negatively associated with the likelihood that 8th- and 9th-graders will eventually enter and complete 12th grade.

The use of standardized testing, along with the resultant system of extrinsic rewards and consequences, has had a negative effect on students' motivation. As a result, students' fear of failure has lessened their motivation to learn.

Testing Does Not Lead to Learning

Given the fact that high stakes are now being attached to all standardized tests, the amount of pressure placed upon children, teachers, and administrators to perform is overwhelming. When increased pressure is placed on individuals to perform, they naturally resort to doing the things that will earn the swiftest reward—in this case, higher test scores. But what does this mean for children's learning? Are children learning more today because of mandated tests?

Although each president since Lyndon Johnson has implemented some type of education package that included standardized tests and claimed its future success in creating better schools for our nation's children, little evidence exists that children's learning has actually improved because of these tests. [Researchers Audrey L.] Amrein and [David C.] Berliner (2003) posited that if students were showing an increase in learning based on state tests, they should show an increase in learning on other independent measures as well. Those researchers examined four student achievement measures—the SAT, the ACT, advanced placement (AP) tests, and the National Assessment of Educational Progress (NAEP)—in 18 states. What they found, in terms of a connection to learning, was virtually nothing. "Nothing seemed to be happening on these measures of student learning. In fact, we can make a strong case that high stakes testing policies hurt student learning instead of helping it." A study by Nichols, Glass, and Berliner (2005) also indicates a weak correlation between high-stakes testing and learning. While they found some validity to the claim that math achievement increased as pressure from high-stakes tests became more prevalent, their findings also indicated that increased testing pressure produced no gains in reading scores at the 4th- or 8th-grade level when students took the National Assessment of Educational Progress (NAEP).

Although those in power would have us believe that increased testing motivates students to learn more, research indicates that the correlation is weak at best and non-existent at worst. Testing does virtually nothing to support or increase student learning.

Limiting and Narrowing the Curriculum

High-stakes testing not only negatively affects motivation and learning, it also undermines the curriculum. Because of the increased pressure on teachers for their children to do well on standardized tests, the curriculum has been narrowed. The curriculum, and thus instructional time, has shifted to only those areas that are to be tested. In many instances, the time given to art, music, creative writing, physical education, and recess has either been reduced or dropped altogether in favor of more intensive drilling on the test subjects. With the advent of Reading First grants, specific curriculum and materials used to teach are now being mandated, which narrows the curriculum even further. Low-performing schools can apply for these federal monies; in order to receive the grant, however, the schools must use government-approved materials and teachers must be trained by government-approved providers. No longer is teachers' professional judgment about curriculum and instruction valued. It has been replaced with curriculum deemed valuable by the federal government as a means to achieving high scores on standardized tests.

Teachers report that the pressure to do well on the tests hinders their instructional practice. They are forced to teach in ways that are not developmentally appropriate and do not promote critical thinking and decision-making. Rather, instruction has become mundane and boring as children complete worksheets on basic facts and memorize items for the test. Instruction has been reduced to teaching to the test. The very instructional strategies that should be used to create and promote democratic values in the classroom are now replaced with mundane skill-drill-kill exercises whereby children do not think for themselves, critically examine possibilities, or take risks. The very heart of democracy has been stripped from our public schools in the name of high-stakes test scores. . . .

An Inappropriate Tool for Education

This position paper from the Association for Childhood Education International denounces the continued use of standardized testing in the primary grades and cautions against the use of these tests as a sole means of assessment in every year throughout the upper grades. Standardized tests are inappropriate to future learning and the motivation to learn. They have taken away the power of classroom teachers to make informed decisions about instruction and learning that leads to critical thinking, higher level learning, and decision-making. Standardized tests have forced teachers to resort to skill-drill teaching, which results in monotonous rote memorization. To continue such testing in the face of so much evidence of its detrimental effects in regards to motivation to learn, learning itself, and the narrowing of curriculum is irresponsible and inappropriate.

"Caring, effective teachers should want to prepare their students for . . . future testing situations."

Standardized Testing Is a Useful Tool Within Public Schools

Linda Crocker

Linda Crocker contends in the following viewpoint that effective test preparation does not result in a narrowing of curriculum or "teaching to the test." She argues that the skills that aid students in passing standardized assessments are also applicable in many situations in both the classroom and society at large. Therefore, caring educators should want to teach and reinforce these skills, Crocker contends. Linda Crocker coauthored the book Introduction to Classical and Modern Test Theory.

As you read, consider the following questions:

1. What national program that utilizes a core curriculum and standardized testing does Crocker refer to as being successful and generating minimum controversy?

2. According to the author, what are the four essential elements of teaching for assessment?

3. After reviewing the list of pointers for effective test preparation, what benefits of this method of teaching become obvious, according to Crocker?

designed to cause destruction

One flashpoint in the incendiary debate over standardized testing in American public schools is the area of test preparation. As noted by [Jeffrey K.] Smith, [Lisa F.] Smith, and [Richard] DeLisi (2001), "we exist in an era in which student testing and the rigorous standards associated with testing seem to be the educational position of choice amongst politicians. Test scores have become the coin of the realm in education, and with that, concerns about how to get students to do well on tests has risen." Critics of standardized testing often voice at least two types of concern about test preparation:

1. Test preparation requires drilling students on a narrow set of low-level skills covered on the test, ignoring material that would have been covered had the teacher been unfettered by demands of preparing students for the assessment.

2. Instruction aimed at making students skillful test-takers on standardized assessments may be harmful to their educational development and thinking processes. . . .

Benefits of Teaching Test-Taking Skills

Many teachers view teaching of test-taking skills as a tawdry practice. They may avoid it or undertake instruction geared to preparing students to demonstrate their knowledge in a particular format—multiple choice, essay, and performance assessment—in a shamefaced or clandestine fashion. This unfortunate situation, largely engendered by critics of standardized testing, impedes student performance and harms teacher morale. Yet, more than 20 years ago, [educator Irving P.] McPhail (1981) offered two worthy reasons for teaching test-taking skills: (a) "to improve the validity of test results" and (b) "to provide equal educational, employment, and promotional opportunity" particularly for disadvantaged students who often do not have access to additional educational resources enjoyed by their middle-class cohorts. This rationale remains compelling today.

In the highly mobile twenty-first century, students migrate with their parents across state and national borders, attend colleges thousands of miles from home, and apply for employment and graduate or professional studies in areas where their transcripts and other credentials cannot be measured on a common metric by those making the selection decisions. Standardized tests have become critical tools for decisions regarding college admission, college credits for high school work, graduate or school professional admission, and licensure for many blue-collar and white-collar professions. Put simply, no one becomes a physician, lawyer, teacher, nurse, accountant, electrician, firefighter, cosmetologist, or real estate broker without taking a series of tests. Caring, effective teachers should want to prepare their students for these future testing situations.

Furthermore the test-taking skills required by the short-essay or performance assessments, which now accompany the objective-item formats of many standardized assessments, have additional application to many real-world contexts in which individuals encounter demands for spontaneous written communications. Consider, for example, the following requests: "Explain why you have come to the clinic today and describe your symptoms"; "Describe how the accident occurred, and use diagrams, if necessary"; or "Describe your qualifications for the position." The ability to respond to a set of structured questions in a specific format has become a communications skill that is as vital in the repertoire of today's student as rhetoric was to the student of the nineteenth century. It is certainly as appropriate for teachers to impart these skills to students as it is for them to instruct them in other forms of oral and written communication. . . .

Prescribed Curriculum at Work

By contrast, a large-scale testing program that generally has generated minimal controversy is the Advanced Placement (AP) program, administered by ETS [Educational Testing Service], in which tests are used for awarding college credit to students on the basis of high school course work. Since the 1950s, a variety of AP high school courses have been created through cooperative efforts of university and secondary education faculty for the purpose of providing junior and senior high school students the opportunity to study introductory level college coursework prior to high school graduation. The course curricula are aligned to standardized assessments, administered at year end or semester end, with substantial stakes for individual students, in the form of college credit for those who receive a prespecified score. Teachers of AP courses plan and deliver instruction in their own ways, but their syllabi are designed to fit the core AP curriculum and they must cover material on schedule to ensure that their students are prepared by the date of the test. AP teachers have access to practice tests and their students generally participate in multiple practice test sessions. The AP assessments, consisting of both multiple choice and constructed response exercises, are developed and scored by ETS, and distributed to universities designated by the student.

More than 70% of the high schools in 23 states offer AP courses; in an additional 11 states, 50% to 69% of the high schools offer such courses; only four states offer AP courses in fewer than 25% of their high schools. This popular, long-established instructional and testing program provides a strong counterexample to testing critics' fears. It demonstrates that a prescribed curriculum coupled with an externally administered end-of-course assessment per se does not automatically result in drill-and-practice instruction, avoidance of challenging subject material, or mind-numbing assignments. . . .

Aligning the Curriculum, Not Reducing It

Teaching "to" the test has a negative connotation among teachers, students, and school administrators. It generally refers to targeting and delivering instruction geared solely at the content or format of a particular test for the express purpose of increasing examinee scores. It implies that improvements in test score performance may not represent corresponding increases in knowledge of the broader universe of content that is sampled by the test specifications and test items.

Teaching for assessment . . . has a broader connotation. It refers to teaching students the broader content domain represented by the curricular standards, not simply to that subset of content sampled by the items on a single test form. Four essential elements of teaching for the assessment include (a) a challenging core curriculum, (b) comprehensive instruction in that curriculum, (c) developing students' test-taking skills, and (d) adherence to ethical guidelines regarding preparation of students for assessment. . . .

One of the greatest fears of testing opponents is that with high-stakes assessments, teachers will be shackled to teaching content that is easily tested in restricted formats, and forced to subvert their professional judgment and restrict their efforts to covering only that content likely to appear on high-stakes tests at the expense of more comprehensive student learning. This latter view has given rise to such phrases as *curricular reductionism, measurement-driven curriculum.* Many accountability advocates, however, are comfortable with the notion that standardized achievement tests, particularly those tied to state-developed curricular standards, legitimately should play a vital role in shaping curricular and instructional practice. As one district level assessment expert noted, "Often you will hear teachers complain that they have to teach something be-

Regular Assessment Leads to Effective Remediation

Breast cancer is a major concern among women and the physicians who care for them (not to mention the men, women, and children who love and rely upon them). If detected early, breast cancer can be essentially "cured" via minimally invasive treatments. If allowed to metastasize, breast cancer at least disfigures and often kills. Regular mammograms are an effective instrument for the early detection of breast cancer. However, because they are expensive, are somewhat painful, and can generate unnecessary anxiety due to occasional false positive readings, a debate continues in the medical community regarding how "at risk" women should be before they start to receive regular mammograms. In my gender-limited experience, I am somewhat baffled by that debate. There isn't a significant woman in my life—wife, mother, or sister—who does not want to receive regular mammograms even at a relatively early age. When early detection can mean the difference between life and death, academic disputes become somewhat moot. . . .

Patrick J. Wolf, Peabody Journal of Education, *2007.*

cause it is on the test. If a test is the only reason that students are taught concepts such as graphing data, writing hypotheses, genres in literature, or the Pythagorean theorem, then thank goodness for tests!" Their comfort arises from the notion of curricular alignment and its distinction from measurement-driven instruction. Most accountability advocates would view curriculum alignment as desirable, but would view measurement-driven instruction as abdication of professional responsibility.

Curricular alignment is the process of selecting or developing an assessment to ensure that test objectives and exercises are representative of the content domain defined by a prescribed curriculum or set of objectives. It also refers to systematic adaptation of a classroom curriculum to include specific content objectives covered on an assessment. By contrast, *measurement-driven instruction* emphasizes specific content or processes solely because that material is likely to be included on a particular assessment, while de-emphasizing other important aspects of the curriculum that are untested. Unfortunately in practice, the boundary between beneficial curriculum alignment and detrimental measurement-driven instruction is often ambiguous.

Teaching for Learning and the Test

It is noteworthy that, despite the great concerns about measurement-driven instruction, after reviewing empirical research literature, both [educator and testing expert William A.] Mehrens (1998) and [professor of education Gregory J.] Cizek (2002) found relatively sparse evidence to support the claims of negative consequences of classroom teachers' test preparation on student learning. However, when [public policy expert Brian M.] Stecher (2002) also found "little evidence about the extent of negative coaching," he suggested this may be due "in part because it is so difficult to detect." He maintained that mounting evidence of score inflation suggests widespread curricular alignment and coaching practices with potential negative consequences.

A continuum of approaches to test preparation, offered by Smith et al. (2001), is useful to classroom teachers in differentiating curriculum alignment from measurement-driven instruction. The first four stages of this continuum are as follows:

1. Teach . . . without paying attention to the standardized test and hope that the students' abilities will show through on the assessment.

2. Spend most of your time in instruction as you normally do, but spend some time going over item formats to be found on the assessment so that students will be familiar with these formats. . . .

3. Analyze the content of the assessment, make certain that you cover the content in your regular instructional program, then work on item format and test-taking skills as well.

4. Analyze the content of the assessment and restructure your instructional program around that content exclusively. Then in addition engage in Item 3 above. Approach 1 illustrates teaching without test preparation and without curricular alignment. Approach 2 illustrates instruction without curricular alignment, but with some attention to test-taking skills. Approach 4 crosses the line toward measurement-driven instruction. Approach 3 describes a reasonable balance of instruction with curricular alignment and instruction in test-taking skills, especially there is a concerted effort to teach subject-matter knowledge and test-taking skills that will have broad utility to the students beyond this immediate examination situation. Two important caveats of Approach 3 are that (a) the assessment represents a good sample of the core curriculum, and (b) the core curriculum is worthy and important.

Benefits for Students of All Ages

A taxonomy of elements of test-taking skills, developed by [professor Jason] Millman et al. (1965) includes the following categories: time-using strategies, error-avoidance strategies, guessing strategies (that make use of student's partial knowledge), and deductive reasoning strategies. Most well-designed interventions aimed at developing student test-taking skills involve learning and practice activities in all of these categories.

In the 1980s, research on the effectiveness of test preparation strategies for school achievement tests flourished. A substantial meta-analysis, of the effects of 30 controlled studies on coaching for achievement tests, revealed that test preparation programs generally had positive impact on test scores, raising student scores on average by approximately one-quarter standard deviation. Furthermore, the greatest effects were achieved by longer programs that incorporated more opportunities to practice and that were designed to improve broad cognitive skills. Even young children can benefit from appropriate instruction in test-taking strategies. For example, [C.] Callenbach (1973) devised a treatment requiring second graders to listen to oral directions over an extended period of time, understand the directions, ask for clarification if confused, and mark an answer booklet according to directions, which resulted in a positive effect of nearly one-quarter of a standard deviation for students receiving the instruction.

Effective Test Preparation Aids Learning

Test preparation and good teaching can go hand in hand. Development of good test-taking skills is not a frenzied activity to be tackled just prior to administration of a major assessment, but rather a yearlong activity to be incorporated into classroom instruction throughout the year for greatest effectiveness. A compilation of illustrative suggestions for test preparation from a sampling of sources is provided:

1. Always demonstrate a positive attitude in talking with students and parents about tests;

2. Build concentration endurance in test-like conditions over the course of a year, working from shorter to longer tests until students can work for the length of test standardized test period without becoming fatigued or distracted;

3. Practice listening to and reading instructions similar to those used on standardized tests, working sample items, and asking questions if they do not understand the directions;

4. Occasionally use separate answer sheets that require bubbling or circling the correct response;

5. Review responses to practice tests and explain why incorrect answers are incorrect;

6. Provide students with practice on timed tests and teach them how to be self-monitoring in using their time wisely;

7. Model good problem-solving strategies when demonstrating how to approach test items;

8. Talk through the problems to help students learn how to determine what question the item is really asking;

9. Encourage students to explain how they arrived at correct answers;

10. Teach students different ways that questions can be posed (e.g., inclusion of irrelevant information, backward thinking);

11. Provide practice with a variety of item formats;

12. Vary item difficulty to expose students to challenging items. This gives them practice in continuing to work through a test even if they encounter items that they cannot answer.

13. Have students practice systematic strategies for choosing one best answer for multiple-choice items (e.g., eliminate obviously incorrect responses and compare remaining responses. Select response that most closely addresses the question, not simply a response that contains true information that is irrelevant to the question.);

14. Have students practice in reviewing their item responses and deciding when response change is indicated;

15. Grade homework and classwork diagnostically, being on the lookout for individual student response patterns that should be corrected before testing. For example, does Sarah frequently miscopy numbers in setting up math problems? Does James not label his diagrams? Does Marty only complete the first step of a two-stage problem? Does Sue often focus on irrelevant information in the paragraph?

16. Teach students to check on the reasonableness of answers to math problems. If possible, the numeric solution should be inserted into a sentence to answer the question (e.g., "Mary washed _____ cars.") to see if it makes sense;

17. Build students' test-taking vocabulary, using terms that they are likely to encounter on tests in various disciplines. For example, in eighth-grade mathematics, students should be able to read and comprehend terms such as *digit, numeral, quotient, remainder, direction, fraction, decimal, sum, difference, estimate,* and *multiply.* Do not assume that students will recognize a word in print, simply because they recognize its meaning orally. For example, many high school students hear and understand the word *genre* in English class, but fail to recognize it in print.

18. Give students practice on various types of tasks that test exercises may present. For example, some math problems require the student to specify only the correct operation, others require solving the problems, and still others require identification of an error in a solution. Even simple variations such as vertical or linear set-ups of computational problems should be practiced.

19. Teach students the types of phrases commonly used in reading items that require inferences or conclusions from reading passages rather than simply factual information, so that they do not spend valuable time reading and rereading trying to locate an answer which is implied but not specifically stated.

20. For performance assessment items, explain how score rubrics are used to award points and provide students with examples of responses to practice items that would generate full, partial, or no credit. Help students learn to evaluate their own responses.

Upon reviewing this list of recommended practices, four points seem obvious. First, development of good test-taking skills is not limited to low-level content or basic cognitive processes. These generic skills are as applicable in elementary mathematics as they are in AP calculus or twelfth-grade English. Second, students who develop good testing skills also acquire a repertoire of problem-solving skills that will enhance study habits and future learning. Third, good test-taking skills are not a "bag of tricks" enabling students who know nothing about the content domain to achieve high scores. Rather, these skills allow students to demonstrate what they know (or do not know) about the material without interfering "noise" in the scores resulting from lack of familiarity with the assessment format. Finally, instruction in test-taking skills should be grounded in content, offering practice and reinforcement in application of newly acquired content knowledge.

| "No one benefits from . . . radical
reegregation."

Ignoring the Mandates of
Brown v. Board of Education
Will Harm Public Schools

Theodore M. Shaw and Lee C. Bollinger

Theodore M. Shaw and Lee C. Bollinger argue in the following viewpoint that the Brown v. Board of Education *ruling and its accompanying mandates continue to provide important guidelines to ensure that practices of segregation are not re-established in the public education system. For this reason, both authors worry that two Supreme Court rulings pending in 2007 might allow certain school districts to ban voluntary desegregation programs and therefore could potentially undo the progress the* Brown *ruling has made. On June 28, 2007, the Supreme Court ruled, as the authors feared, that the school districts could not be compelled to integrate schools by dictating what schools the students may attend for the sole purpose of racial balancing. Theodore M. Shaw serves as director-council and president of the National Association for the Advancement of Colored People's*

Theodore M. Shaw and Lee C. Bollinger, "The Future of Diversity and Affirmative Action," *New York Amsterdam News*, vol. 98, May 10, 2007, pp. 13–44. Reproduced by permission.

Legal and Educational Defense Fund, and Lee C. Bollinger is the current president of Columbia University in the City of New York.

As you read, consider the following questions:

1. According to the statistics cited by the authors, what percentage of White students attend multiracial schools, and what percent of black and Latino students attend segregated schools?

2. Since the *Brown v. Board of Education* ruling, what is the only thing that Shaw and Bollinger say the courts have made clear in defining what local school districts cannot do?

3. What are some of the problems that could arise from measures passed to dismantle affirmative action, as Shaw and Bollinger contend?

On May 17, we ... honor the ... anniversary of *Brown v. Board of Education*, when the Supreme Court, pressed by Thurgood Marshall [lawyer who argued before the Supreme Court in the *Brown v. Board of Education* victory and eventually became the first African American Supreme Court Justice], shook the pillars of segregation in announcing its new and resounding principle that "separate is inherently unequal." This May [in 2007] is once again a month of reckoning; and as much as we would like to celebrate this shared past, we must also remain vigilant as the Court gets ready to issue opinions in two public school cases that threaten to chip away at *Brown*'s legacy of racial justice and diversity. If successful, both cases—*Parents Involved in Community Schools v. Seattle School District No.1* and *Crystal Meredith v. Jefferson County Board of Education*—will ban local districts from implementing voluntary desegregation programs that seek to maintain racial balance in our schools while countering the worst re-segregation crisis we have faced since the early days of the civil rights movement.

The stakes could not be higher; and with [Justice] Samuel Alito's recent replacement of [Justice] Sandra Day O'Connor—who authored the majority opinions in *Gratz v. Bollinger* and *Grutter v. Bollinger* (2003) affirming the importance of diversity as a compelling justification for affirmative action—the outcome could not be more uncertain.

Segregation Continues

The numbers are disturbing. According to the 2000 census, only 14% of White students attend multiracial schools (schools with at least three races each representing 10% or more of the total student population), while nearly 40% of both Black and Latino students attend intensely segregated schools with a 90–100% minority student population. These figures are inextricably linked to economic segregation. Nationally, almost 50% of all Black and Latino students attend schools in which three-quarters or more of students are poor, compared to only 5% of White students; and in schools of extreme poverty, 80% of the students are Black and Latino.

No one benefits from such radical re-segregation. The isolation of White students prevents them from learning with and from those with different backgrounds—making it more difficult for them to understand those who are different from themselves or to learn how to thrive in racially diverse settings as adults. Conversely, minority students in segregated schools encounter weaker academic offerings and are too often cut off from integrated networks that improve access to jobs and college admission. Not surprisingly, the nation's high dropout rate crisis is concentrated in segregated high schools in big cities.

Undoing the Victory of *Brown v. Board of Education*

The K–12 voluntary integration programs before the Court attempt to remedy this situation. Adopted by local, democratically-elected school boards, these initiatives represent a milestone in the nation's long and arduous quest to achieve *Brown*'s core principle—equal opportunity.

Yet at oral arguments in December [2006] detractors urged the Court to apply the "strict scrutiny" test it had outlined in the affirmative action cases we argued, because, they maintained, it is unfair for school officials to consider race when assigning students within a district—even if it is done to achieve the very goals of integration that *Brown* envisioned.

This is a perverse reading of the Court's jurisprudence. Worse, it threatens to unravel everything for which *Brown* stands. While the Court in *Brown* was emphatic in outlawing the use of race for segregative purposes, it never suggested that race-conscious integrative student assignments violated the Equal Protection Clause. To do so would have undermined its efforts to heal the Jim Crow America that *Plessy* [landmark Supreme Court ruling in *Plessy v. Ferguson* deeming racial segregation constitutional] had legitimized decades before.

Since then, courts have been clear that local school districts have every freedom to implement integration programs that go beyond the constitutional floor that *Brown* established in 1954. The only thing they may not do is slide back toward segregation.

Recent Legislation Undermines Integration

Today, in many school districts across the country—including those before the current Court—voluntary integration programs have become the last best hope for overcoming just that: intense residential segregation and concentrated poverty. It is not too much to say that they represent all that is left of *Brown*.

Yet these cases are not the only challenges we face in education today. In fact, as soon as the ink dried on the Court's

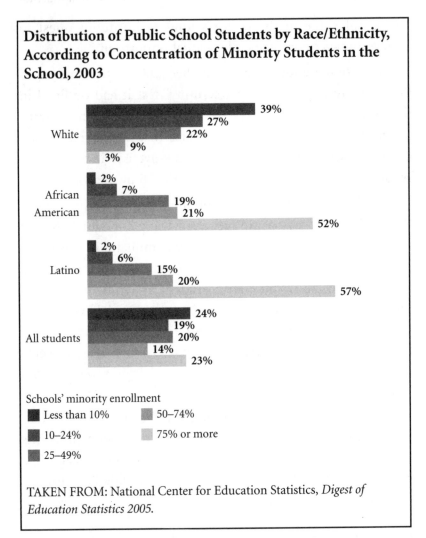

Distribution of Public School Students by Race/Ethnicity, According to Concentration of Minority Students in the School, 2003

White
- 39%
- 27%
- 22%
- 9%
- 3%

African American
- 2%
- 7%
- 19%
- 21%
- 52%

Latino
- 2%
- 6%
- 15%
- 20%
- 57%

All students
- 24%
- 19%
- 20%
- 14%
- 23%

Schools' minority enrollment
- ■ Less than 10%
- ■ 10–24%
- ■ 25–49%
- ■ 50–74%
- ■ 75% or more

TAKEN FROM: National Center for Education Statistics, *Digest of Education Statistics 2005.*

opinions upholding affirmative action as a constitutional matter, its opponents scrambled to undo it. Unfortunately, they appear to be succeeding.

Just last November [2006], a majority of voters in Michigan joined California and Washington as the third state to pass a ballot measure to dismantle all public affirmative action programs. Doing so assures that their great public universities will become less diverse. As a result, they also become less attractive options for potential students who recognize that living and studying with classmates from a diverse range of backgrounds is essential training for an increasingly global world—one that rewards those with the instinct to reach out instead of clinging to the comforts of what seems natural or familiar.

It is also vital for establishing a cohesive, truly national society—one in which rising generations learn to overcome the biases they absorb as children while also appreciating the unique talents their colleagues bring to any equation. Only education can get us there. As Thurgood Marshall knew so well: "The law can open doors and knock down walls, but it cannot build bridges. We will only attain freedom if we learn to appreciate what is different and muster the courage to discover what is fundamentally the same."

All of this is under siege now. At the elementary and secondary school levels, re-segregation is making it exceedingly difficult for minority students to access the resources that inspire rising generations to apply to and then attend college. At the same time, the elimination of affirmative action programs at our public universities is keeping admissions officials from lifting these same students up in order to offset the structural inequalities they had to face in getting there. . . .

In these times, it is easy for ordinary people to wonder if they can make a tangible difference in the long struggle for justice. Yet as uncertain as the future feels at this moment, the history of this month reminds us that good things happen when ordinary citizens—like Oliver Brown and the other parents of Topeka, Kansas, who contacted their local NAACP [National Association for the Advancement of Colored People] chapter all those years ago—come together to listen, talk, and work together for an America of true equal opportunity.

> *"During the last 20 years, with* Brown
> *in full force, America's public schools
> have been growing more segregated."*

Moving Beyond the Mandates of *Brown v. Board of Education* Will Improve Public Schools

Juan Williams

Juan Williams is a senior correspondent for National Public Radio and a political analyst for Fox News Channel. In the following viewpoint, Williams contends that while the Supreme Court's 1954 decision in Brown v. Board of Education *to desegregate schools was noble, it has not ensured that every child in America has the same opportunity to attend a free public school. He praises the Supreme Court for its June 28, 2007, decision to allow school districts in Seattle, Washington, and Louisville, Kentucky, to ban the redistricting of students solely for the purpose of balancing the racial makeup of individual schools, stating that focusing on having racial percentages balanced allows policymakers to ignore low minority graduation rates and other problems that plague the education system.*

As you read, consider the following questions:

1. What percentage of black and Hispanic students drop out of high school, according to the author?

2. What examples does Williams give to show the way that the *Brown v. Board of Education* decision became less relevant starting in the early 1990s?

3. According to Williams, how did Justice Thurgood Marshall respond to the question of whether he had made a mistake by insisting on racial integration of public schools?

L et us now praise the *Brown* decision. Let us now bury the *Brown* decision.

With [the] Supreme Court ruling ending the use of voluntary schemes to create racial balance among students, it is time to acknowledge that *Brown*'s time has passed. It is worthy of a send-off with fanfare for setting off the civil rights movement and inspiring social progress for women, gays and the poor. But the decision in *Brown v. Board of Education* that focused on outlawing segregated schools as unconstitutional is now out of step with American political and social realities.

The Failure of Integration

Desegregation does not speak to dropout rates that hover near 50 percent for black and Hispanic high school students. It does not equip society to address the so-called achievement gap between black and white students that mocks *Brown*'s promise of equal educational opportunity.

And the fact is, during the last 20 years, with *Brown* in full force, America's public schools have been growing more segregated—even as the nation has become more racially diverse. In 2001, the National Center for Education Statistics reported that the average white student attends a school that is 80 percent white, while 70 percent of black students attend schools where nearly two-thirds of students are black and Hispanic.

By the early '90s, support in the federal courts for the central work of *Brown*—racial integration of public schools—began to rapidly expire. In a series of cases in Atlanta, Oklahoma City and Kansas City, Mo., frustrated parents, black and white, appealed to federal judges to stop shifting children from school to school like pieces on a game board. The parents wanted better neighborhood schools and a better education for their children, no matter the racial makeup of the school. In their rulings ending court mandates for school integration, the judges, too, spoke of the futility of using schoolchildren to address social ills caused by adults holding fast to patterns of residential segregation by both class and race.

The focus of efforts to improve elementary and secondary schools shifted to magnet schools, to allowing parents the choice to move their children out of failing schools and, most recently, to vouchers and charter schools. The federal No Child Left Behind plan has many critics, but there's no denying that it is an effective tool for forcing teachers' unions and school administrators to take responsibility for educating poor and minority students.

A Decision for Another Time

It was an idealistic Supreme Court that in 1954 approved of *Brown* as a race-conscious policy needed to repair the damage of school segregation and protect every child's Fourteenth Amendment right to equal treatment under law. In 1971, Chief Justice Warren Burger, writing for a unanimous court still embracing *Brown*, said local school officials could make racial integration a priority even if it did not improve educational outcomes because it helped "to prepare students to live in a pluralistic society."

To Stop Discrimination, Stop Discriminating

As counsel who appeared before [the U.S. Supreme] Court for the plaintiffs in Brown [v. Board of Education] put it: "We have one fundamental contention which we will seek to develop in the course of this argument, and that contention is that no State has any authority under the equal-protection clause of the Fourteenth Amendment to use race as a factor in affording educational opportunities among its citizens." There is no ambiguity in that statement. And it was that position that prevailed in this Court, which emphasized in its remedial opinion that what was "[a]t stake is the personal interest of the plaintiffs in admission to public schools as soon as practicable *on a nondiscriminatory basis*," and what was required was "determining admission to the public schools *on a nonracial basis*." What do the racial classifications do in these cases [*Parents Involved in Community Schools v. Seattle School District No. 1* and *Crystal D. Meredith v. Jefferson County Board of Education*], if not determine admission to a public school on a racial basis? Before *Brown*, schoolchildren were told where they could and could not go to school based on the color of their skin. The school districts in these cases have not carried the heavy burden of demonstrating that we should allow this once again—even for very different reasons. For schools that never segregated on the basis of race, such as Seattle, or that have removed the vestiges of past segregation, such as Jefferson County, the way "to achieve a system of determining admission to the public schools on a nonracial basis," is to stop assigning students on a racial basis. The way to stop discrimination on the basis of race is to stop discriminating on the basis of race.

Opinion of the U.S. Supreme Court in Parents Involved in Community Schools v. Seattle School District No. 1 *and* Crystal D. Meredith v. Jefferson County Board of Education, *June 28, 2007.*

But today a high court with a conservative majority concludes that any policy based on race—no matter how well intentioned—is a violation of every child's Fourteenth Amendment right to be treated as an individual without regard to race. We've come full circle.

In 1990, after months of interviews with Justice Thurgood Marshall, who had been the lead lawyer for the N.A.A.C.P. [National Association for the Advancement of Colored People] Legal Defense Fund on the *Brown* case, I sat in his Supreme Court chambers with a final question. Almost 40 years later, was he satisfied with the outcome of the decision? Outside the courthouse, the failing Washington school system was hypersegregated, with more than 90 percent of its students black and Latino. Schools in the surrounding suburbs, meanwhile, were mostly white and producing some of the top students in the nation.

Had Mr. Marshall, the lawyer, made a mistake by insisting on racial integration instead of improvement in the quality of schools for black children?

His response was that seating black children next to white children in school had never been the point. It had been necessary only because all-white school boards were generously financing schools for white children while leaving black students in overcrowded, decrepit buildings with hand-me-down books and underpaid teachers. He had wanted black children to have the right to attend white schools as a point of leverage over the biased spending patterns of the segregationists who ran schools—both in the 17 states where racially separate schools were required by law and in other states where they were a matter of culture.

If black children had the right to be in schools with white children, Justice Marshall reasoned, then school board officials would have no choice but to equalize spending to protect the interests of their white children.

New Policies for a Global Society

Racial malice is no longer the primary motive in shaping inferior schools for minority children. Many failing big city schools today are operated by black superintendents and mostly black school boards.

And today the argument that school reform should provide equal opportunity for children, or prepare them to live in a pluralistic society, is spent. The winning argument is that better schools are needed for all children—black, white, brown and every other hue—in order to foster a competitive workforce in a global economy.

Dealing with racism and the bitter fruit of slavery and "separate but equal" legal segregation was at the heart of the court's brave decision 53 years ago. With *Brown* officially relegated to the past, the challenge for brave leaders now is to deliver on the promise of a good education for every child.

Periodical Bibliography

The following articles have been selected to supplement the diverse views presented in this chapter.

American School Board Journal	"The Condition of Education," August 2007.
Erling E. Boe and Sujie Shin	"Is the United States Really Losing the International Horse Race in Academic Achievement?" *Phi Delta Kappan*, May 2005.
Lee C. Bollinger	"Why Diversity Matters," *Chronicle of Higher Education*, June 1, 2007.
Zoë Burkholder	"'Because Race Can't Be Ignored,'" *Education Week*, October 24, 2007.
Diverse: Issues in Higher Education	"Report: U.S. Students More Prepared Academically than 20 Years Ago," August 25, 2005.
Rick Ginsberg and Leif Frederick Lyche	"The Culture of Fear and the Politics of Education," *Educational Policy*, January 2008.
William B. Harvey	"The Weakest Link: A Commentary on the Connections Between K–12 and Higher Education," *American Behavioral Scientist*, March 2008.
J. Amos Hatch	"Learning as a Subversive Activity," *Phi Delta Kappan*, December 2007.
New York Times	"Resegregation Now," June 29, 2007.
Peter Schrag	"Schoolhouse Crock," *Harper's*, September 2007.
USA Today Magazine	"Schools Appear Ready to Resegregate," September 2007.
Wall Street Journal	"Worse Than You Think," October 24, 2007.

OPPOSING
VIEWPOINTS®
SERIES

Chapter 2

Are Alternatives to Public Education Viable?

Chapter Preface

Charter schools are products of late 1980s thinking and early 1990s legislation. Pushed forward by educators who wanted to reform the public school system—especially in economically depressed areas of the country—charter schools were devised under the belief that freeing educators from some of the demands of school districts and state governments would allow them to focus on innovative teaching approaches that could generate better student performance. The school administration signs a charter with the school district for a specific term (perhaps five years) in which it will receive public funds in exchange for anticipated academic results. The results are often measured by standardized achievement testing, and if these results are not met, the school's charter may be revoked. State legislators believed that because of the emphasis on verifiable results, charter schools would prove or disprove their worth rather quickly.

In 1991 only Minnesota had adopted a charter school law, but within three years the number of states with such laws jumped to eleven. In 2008 charter school laws are on the books in forty states and the District of Columbia. Though popular, charter schools have struggled to meet expectations. National assessments by the Department of Education have revealed that students attending charter schools are not measuring up academically to peers in the public system. Standardized test scores have been slightly below average in their districts. However, charter advocates suggest that these results might be explained by other factors not related to attending a charter school. They also point to other recorded benefits of charters such as better student attendance and improved student behavior—problems that plague public schools in disadvantaged areas. Giving power and choice to poorer students and parents is one of the primary reasons the George W. Bush administration strongly supports charter schools. As Secretary of Education Margaret Spellings argued in 2006, "Charter schools are empowering low-income parents with new educational options and providing an important lifeline for families in areas where traditional public schools have fallen short of their responsibilities."

Because charter schools must ultimately be judged by student progress, critics assert that these schools do not empower all low-income families. Some have charged that charter schools select students who are most likely to succeed, leaving many underprivileged and undereducated children trapped in failing public schools. These critics also point out that children trapped in public schools suffer because money is drawn away from their schools to pay for the select students who will attend charter schools. Supporters of charter schools, on the other hand, argue that when the marketplace shows public schools that parents are willing to remove their children from poor educational settings, the public schools will be forced to come up with new ideas—and improved learning environments—to compete. In this way, the market of options will help satisfy all parents and students.

In the following chapter, analysts and educators examine other proposed alternatives to the current public school system such as tuition vouchers for families that cannot afford private education or same-sex school options.

"Allowing consumers to choose and suppliers to compete would improve education."

Privatizing Education Would Be Beneficial

Mark Harrison

In the following viewpoint, Mark Harrison, a freelance economist and consultant in Australia, states that the American public school system has failed teachers, students, and parents. He contends that privatizing schools would introduce competition, forcing school administrations to hire better teachers, reward exemplary performance, embrace innovations, and improve student outcomes. To Harrison, privatization would also allow parents to choose better schools for their children and base their selection upon criteria that are important to them.

As you read, consider the following questions:

1. How will teachers' wages be affected under the market-based system Harrison describes?

Mark Harrison, "Public Problems, Private Solutions: School Choice and Its Consequences," *Cato Journal*, vol. 25, Spring-Summer 2005, pp. 203–212.

2. What does Harrison believe will be necessary to promote housing desegregation so that schools can bolster socioeconomic diversity?

3. According to Harrison, in what way will privatization bring about greater parental involvement in the school system?

The key to improving the education system is to move away from public provision to a decentralized competitive market—where families can choose between competing, specialized, autonomous suppliers. A market system would overcome many of the problems with public provision. Giving parents the freedom to choose will benefit both parents and the education system. It would boost educational innovation, lift up the poor, encourage better teaching, and promote parental involvement.

Market Reform Will Create Choice

A market system moves decisionmaking from government agencies to the family and to the school level—where the incentives and information are superior. Schools are directly accountable to parents, rather than indirectly through the political process. Power shifts from producers to consumers. Choice is about abolishing restraints on families and increasing their options—options that families will only take up if they become better off.

The market-based approach relies on choice and competition to increase incentives to perform, improve, and change. The market harnesses self-interest and coordinates widespread knowledge to deliver better services at a lower cost than government provision. Decentralized decisionmaking makes sense because individuals have the strongest incentive and best information to further their own interests.

Market accountability means that parents would determine the menu of education options, but control over individual schools would be in the hands of producers. Schools would have both the autonomy and incentive to dramatically improve schooling. In a market system, schools are free to experiment. Schools can spend more, rely on outside experts, or adopt standards if they think that will improve performance and attract students.

Competing schools of choice must attract students to survive, and their viability would depend on seeking out and satisfying market demands. Specialized offerings would meet parents' preferences. Schools running themselves and being directly accountable to parents would, in general, lead to the best results for children. . . .

Incentives for Efficiency and Diversity

A market arrangement uses competition, choice, the price mechanism, and the profit motive to provide incentives and coordinate behavior so as to use available resources for their most valuable purposes, as judged by consumer willingness to pay. Freedom to choose checks the power of the state, allows for diversity, and encourages suppliers to develop and adopt innovations that consumers value.

A universal voucher of a substantial amount would give all families the choice of private schooling and would encourage the development of the private sector. A large private sector would provide increased competition for public schools and a source of diversity in educational opportunities. In the absence of outside competition, the government system has little incentive to adopt desirable reforms and is subject to political pressures not to. Even the limited competition sometimes permitted between government schools and between a fringe private sector and a dominant state system improves public school performance. Studies of schools subject to some market incentives (private schools, the for-profit sector, and charter schools) in the United States demonstrate how the market satisfies diverse preferences, stimulates innovation, and has a strong customer focus—often addressing needs neglected by the public system.

Market Accountability Fosters Innovation

Competition in education, as in all markets, enables small-scale experiments. It rewards successful ones and discards unsuccessful ones. Moreover, competition gives rise to pressure for continual improvement, to reduce costs and provide better products—or lose market share to competitors who do these things. Successful practices are quickly copied. Firms have the incentive to experiment with and adapt new approaches and to replace ineffective approaches with better alternatives. Firms that do so will earn higher profits (through more students, higher fees, or lower costs). Firms that do not will earn lower profits, and ultimately their survival will be threatened. Even a private firm with a monopoly faces capital market pressure to improve or risk takeover by someone who can run it better. Competition can force schools to adopt changes that benefit consumers, even if they make producers as a whole worse off.

In a market system, innovations must meet the market test. Innovations will only survive if they are better than the alternatives for at least some consumers. The market gives feedback on, and the incentive to respond to, how consumers value changes. The market involves continual testing against alternatives. It reacts to changing circumstances and permits incremental changes and tradeoffs.

The Market Encourages Good Teaching

A competitive market is likely to change the structure of pay and the type of person attracted to the teaching profession. [Economist Caroline Minter] Hoxby points out that economic theory

> predicts that schools that faced stronger competition would favor teachers who raised the schools' ability to attract stu-

dents. These schools presumably would strive to attract and retain teachers who were especially talented or hard-working or who possessed rare skills. In turn, you would expect their tolerance for less effective teachers to wane. You would expect, in fact, that teaching would be transformed into a true profession, where workers are rewarded not only on the basis of seniority but also on the basis of their skills and performance.

In a market system, wages are likely to be more closely related to performance. The prerequisites are in place—performance of teachers varies widely, and good performance can be measured at the school level (for example, by the principal). The result is likely to be increased salary ranges and rewards for good teaching—which in turn will encourage better teaching.

Performance-related pay would encourage talented individuals to join and stay in the profession. The effectiveness of different compensation arrangements, teacher hiring practices, training methods, and institutional structures would be decided by open competition.

One objection to performance pay is that teaching performance is difficult to measure objectively. Another is that it is difficult to disentangle the effects of previous education, other teachers, and non-school factors. Most workers in the economy are evaluated subjectively, and rewards for good performance are used in many firms where measurement of individual performance is difficult. In many firms, output reflects the contribution of many individuals, and interactions with colleagues are important. In these cases of team production, individual contributions to output cannot be easily identified. In many industries, such as the health industry, outcomes are difficult to measure. Nevertheless, most workers in these areas receive merit rewards, raises, and promotions based on their bosses' subjective evaluation of performance. There is nothing wrong with subjective decisions, so long as the decisionmakers face the correct incentives.

The unions argue that performance pay saps morale by pitting teachers against one another, but it could be argued that it is more demoralizing for a hard-working and accomplished teacher to see a lazy and incompetent colleague getting the same pay—as is often the case under current arrangements.

Teachers Become Accountable for School Performance

In a competitive environment, both management and employees at a school have an incentive to adopt changes that improve productivity in order to survive against competitors or to share in the gains. They must take account of the possibility that competitors will provide a better service at a lower price. Staff members must be concerned about the overall effectiveness of the school and the contribution of colleagues. For example, if performance pay improves the quality of the school's staff, the school improves its reputation, and the demand for its services increases—to the benefit of all staff members.

Under public provision, neither teachers nor management would benefit from an improvement in productivity. Instead, the main concern is about distributional rather than efficiency issues—the amount of spending and the share going to teachers. At the school level, poor performance may lead to additional resources. In public education, once the teaching budget is determined, more for one teacher means less for others. It pits teachers against each other. . . .

Studies of U.S. private schools reveal the effects of managerial autonomy and market accountability in a competitive environment. Private schools have different hiring and compensation policies than public schools. They have better teach-

Public Schools Are Failing America

Millions of American parents have, when they can afford it, chosen to send their kids to private or parochial schools, or even to homeschool them (which is an *incredible* feat and burden) because they don't want their kids dumbed-down to the intelligence level of an amoeba. In short, they want their kids to succeed, and in far too many communities, the public school institution just isn't producing.

Countless recent studies have shown that American students rank well behind western counterparts in math and the sciences. Also, zillions of kids graduate high school but, colleges say, cannot adequately spell or write complete sentences, and cannot understand why they can't do these things because reading comprehension is also abysmal. . . .

That's pathetic; how many more trillions of dollars are we going to pour down the non-productive, scandal-ridden, national teachers' union-influenced public schools before we "figger out" that "shucks, this ain't workin'"?

John Dougherty, "Private American Education,"
WorldNetDaily, February 7, 2001. www.worldnetdaily.com.

ers than public schools because they have policies and an environment that attract good teachers and encourage good teaching. They draw on a larger talent pool by hiring teachers with high ability and strong subject knowledge but without formal teaching credentials. Continued employment depends on classroom performance—private schools dismiss bad teachers. Teachers care greatly about working conditions. Teachers in private schools are more likely to express greater job satisfaction and strong, positive attitudes about their schools.

Market Accountability Helps the Poor

Even the defenders of public education admit that many disadvantaged students are trapped in failed schools. Unsuccessful schools are unlikely to survive in a market. It is not profitable to run schools that no one wants to attend. Poor students present a market opportunity for many for-profit firms precisely because they are neglected by the public system. The market will cater to any group of students if it is profitable to do so, something the government can guarantee with financial support for school choices. It would extend to all the kinds of choices the rich take for granted, which will benefit the poor. Resources will be more useful to poor parents if schools are directly accountable to them.

One criticism of markets is that they are inequitable because they result in stratification by ability, and low-income students without high ability will be isolated and concentrated, their problems exacerbated by adverse peer effects: the worst off become even worse off. There is little evidence that competition would result in greater segregation than under the current system. Zoning reproduces and reinforces segregation in housing and allows the rich to buy their way into good government schools by choice of residence. The evidence is that extending school choice to the poor would likely promote social integration and reduce social polarization. In the early 1990s, dezoning (choice among government schools) in New Zealand, England, and Wales reduced student segregation by socioeconomic status. . . .

Simulations in the United States find that a voucher program would promote housing desegregation by changing residential choices. A voucher program would remove the need for high-income households to leave poor neighborhoods in order to receive better schooling and reduce the difference in real estate prices between areas with better schools and lesser performing alternatives. A voucher severs the link between the choice of where to live and where to send your child to school and so removes the segregating effects of "selection by mortgage."

A market system provides more diversity so that less emphasis is placed on socioeconomic status and race. In fact, it helps bring together new communities. Parents will choose schools where other parents have similar tastes. To the extent they choose on the basis of shared values, special needs, educational philosophy, discipline, religious denominational instruction, single-sex schooling, sports, music, and so on, there will be more sorting according to these tastes and less segregation by income and ability. Specialized private schools will draw people from different backgrounds and neighborhoods. Further, if parents care about social mixing and diversity, they will deliberately choose schools that offer a diverse student body and the opportunity for their children to mix with different types of students.

Market Accountability Boosts Parental Involvement

A further benefit from choice is increased parental involvement and a strengthened role for families. Education is a partnership between family and school. Like any partnership, it works better if the parties choose each other. Parents of children in school choice programs are more involved with their children's academic programs, participate more in school activities, volunteer more in their children's schools, communicate more with teachers, and help more with homework. Greater choice also makes parents more interested in their child's school.

When parents choose to send their children to a school, it implies a level of commitment. Seeking out a suitable school engages parents. Further, paying fees encourages parents to monitor schools more closely. People pay for what they value and value what they pay for.

Greater involvement in schooling by parents makes their children perform better. The benefits to children from having their parents more involved are just as large from parents of low education and income as from parents with more education and income.

The Public School System Has Failed

Public provision has failed. The government does a poor job in providing education, even on criteria such as promoting equity. The problems are inherent in public provision. Those in charge simply do not have the information or incentive to satisfy consumers, control costs, innovate, or encourage good teaching.

Government control of schools is used to achieve political objectives other than the public interest, such as benefiting politically powerful teachers unions and other producer interest groups. The result is to further reduce efficiency and harm the poor.

Choice and competition provide the best setting to unleash human efforts to resolve problems and encourage the ultimate determinants of student performance. Allowing consumers to choose and suppliers to compete would improve education—but the largest benefits would come from a full market system, with free entry and exit to maximize competition and choice. . . .

When the government runs schools, issues that are properly internal management issues are, instead, decided through the political process. Educational issues become political issues. In contrast, in a market system, autonomous school management will make these decisions itself. Success is judged by consumers on the basis of results, rather than through the political process. Competition drives schools to satisfy consumers and improve, something that no amount of tinkering with a public system will provide.

> *"To remove schools from the public sphere and place them in the market would be to deprive democracy of one of the most reliable . . . institutions it has for self-renewal."*

Privatizing Education Would Be Harmful

John F. Covaleskie

John F. Covaleskie is a professor of education at University of Oklahoma. In the following viewpoint, he argues that privatizing education would be harmful to the notion of public good. Covaleskie asserts that public schools are more than just academic institutions; instead, they are public spaces where young citizens are taught the value of public concern, democracy, and the common good. He contends that privatizing education would eliminate this worthwhile agenda, forcing schools to serve private aims that may not agree with public interests.

As you read, consider the following questions:

1. As Covaleskie explains, how does John Dewey define a public?

John F. Covaleskie, "What Public? Whose Schools?" *Educational Studies*, August 2007, pp. 28–29, 34, 37–41. Reproduced by permission of Taylor & Francis, Ltd., http//:www.tandf.co.uk/journals, conveyed through Copyright Clearance Center, Inc., and the author.

2. How have public schools become more beholden to corporate interests, in the author's view?

3. As Covaleskie states, what is "the public good served by public education"?

Discussions about the quality of public schools, the role of public schools, and reform of public schools mostly are about schools, not about the public. In this article I reverse that, paying little attention to the particular features of schools, but attending to the meaning of *public*, especially as it relates to education and schooling.

The several-decades-old attack against the idea of public education is bearing fruit and has little to do with any specific criticism of public schools; the attack is on the idea of public schooling, and the criticisms shift on an ad-hoc basis. This endangers America's democratic experiment. As vouchers gain political traction and the blessing of the Supreme Court, and as the No Child Left Behind Act goes into effect, strongly slanted to encourage privatization, two questions get ignored: (a) What is public about public schools, and (b) is there a public to which these sort of schools refer? If there is no public, then there can be no such thing as public schools. In *The Public and Its Problems* [1927], [philosopher and educational reformer John] Dewey considered the nature of publics and their importance to democratic life. Dewey's crucial insights are that (a) a public is not just a collection of individuals, (b) a public is aware of its existence, and (c) a public is engaged in active identification and solution of common problems.

The question of the meaning of *public* and its importance is not just relevant to education. Indeed, the conservative reaction of the past generation has sought to eliminate from public discourse the very idea of a public; it has sought to undo the public that was formed under Franklin Delano Roosevelt's leadership with his idea that there should be such a thing as public works. The market has been displacing, and

continues to displace, the public—to privatize not just education, but roads, water supplies, social security, immigration
control, and even the occupation of Iraq. In short, the conservative reaction of the last 30 years to the New Deal has not
just been to reduce or eliminate public investment in, and
control of, things that arguably might belong in the market
such as telephone service, utilities, and banking. The goal appears broader: to remove the public from the operation of
facets of social life that have long been understood to be in
the public interest, and therefore properly under public
supervision. . . .

What Makes a Public?

To talk intelligently about public schools and democracy requires that one understand the meaning and operation of a
public. Dewey is helpful in this effort.

What Dewey argued, most directly in *The Public and Its
Problems*, is that there is a thing called a *public*, something
that is in some sense real and able to act. A public is real in
that it is what [French sociologist Emile] Durkheim referred
to as a "*social fact*": "What constitutes social facts are the beliefs, tendencies and practices of the group taken collectively."
Social facts are very fragile; they exist if, and only if, people
believe in them and act accordingly.

In Dewey's view, not any collection of individuals makes a
public; publics require (are?) a democratic polity wherein
which policies and decisions are supposed to be made by the
people, constituted as a public. A public recognizes that there
are common problems, problems that must be discovered and
defined by a process of public reflection and then solved by
common action directed to secure some common good. In a
public, individuals address shared concerns through common
action in which the perspective and interests of each member
is given approximately even weight by all members.

It is the recognition of a common good and common problems that brings a public into being, and that recognition is weakened by a rhetoric that assumes there is no such thing. As the social contract is being reconstructed, there is no common project because there are no citizens; there are variously interacting producers, consumers, competitors, and observers. There is no common interest, only individual ones. Pursuit of common interests would (does) limit pursuit of one's own individual interests. . . .

Specious Claims for Privatization

The question is, can a market constitute a public? I think not, but it can obliterate the public, and that is very bad for democracy.

To place this discussion about the difference between markets and publics in context, one should keep in mind that the relation between markets and publics is at the heart of the debate about vouchers and school choice. The data are distorted to make public schools look far less effective than they are. The antipublic argument is that government schools cannot be improved as long as they hold a monopoly on education; both government and monopolies are inherently ineffective. Competition is the solution to whatever educational inadequacies there are, and the provision of vouchers will create competition. However, the argument actually begins with its conclusion: "government" schools are a bad idea. . . .

This argument is thoroughly specious. In the first place, the supposed monopoly government has over education is fictional; school districts are independent entities, responding to a local board of education made up of elected citizens. Any history of education shows both that on the one hand, ideas for improvement of education disseminate through networks of professionals who constantly seek to improve their performance and effectiveness. On the other hand, these independent professionals in different schools manage to adapt spreading reforms to local conditions, again, with the aim of meeting the needs of the local community and its children.

In addition, the evidence is that private schools, with or without vouchers, do not improve the education provided to a community's children. However, the fact that the criticisms of public education are largely unfounded is not the point here; others have made that argument very effectively. The point here is to understand that the attack is only secondarily on schools; it is primarily directed against the idea of a public. For this reason, it is critical to shift the debate; people must stop arguing about which sort of school is more effective in achieving higher levels of achievement on some sort of test and begin pointing out what will be lost to democratic life if society loses the idea of a public. Society needs to begin talking about what children really need to learn, and how individuals ought to be helping them learn it. . . .

The Democratic Basis of Public Schooling

In Dewey's philosophy of social life, education was the way that each new generation would be prepared to take its place in the on-going discussion about how people ought to live together. To remove schools from the public sphere and place them in the market would be to deprive democracy of one of the most reliable (at least in theory) institutions it has for self-renewal.

The *"public"* in *"public schools"* has multiple and overlapping meanings: (a) the schools are owned by the public; (b) they are paid for by the public; (c) they are governed by the public; (d) they reflect the public will; (e) they are open to the public, i.e., they must take all children, who then attend by right, not privilege; (f) they reflect the public ethos; and (g) they help shape the public that will be in the future. That is, public schools are public in their ownership, funding, access, control, and responsibility. Private schools are none of the above. Even though private schools clearly can, and often do,

Should Students and Parents Be Allowed to Choose a Private School at Public Expense?

National Totals

	'06 %	'05 %	'04 %	'03 %	'02 %	'01 %	'97 %	'93 %
Favor	36	38	42	38	46	34	44	24
Oppose	60	57	54	60	52	64	52	74
Don't know	4	5	4	2	2	2	4	2

TAKEN FROM: Lowell C. Rose and Alec M. Gallup, "38th Annual Phi Delta Kappa/Gallup Poll of the Public's Attitudes toward the Public Schools," *Phi Delta Kappan*, September 2006.

serve the public good, it is a private vision of the public good, and that is what policy initiatives like vouchers are intended to preserve.

[In Dewey's view,] schools are the means by which the public in a democratic society fulfills its responsibilities to its children and the democratic ideal; this is the point about a democratic society wanting for all its children what wise parents want for their own children. He is not justifying this claim with reasoning that one would recognize today. He is not saying that people should take care of their children because they need good education to get good jobs, though he does value education that prepares people for productive lives. Still less does he mean that education is a prudent investment in the productivity of the future workers on whom one's social security check will depend, although he would certainly grant the truth of that claim as well. No, for Dewey the goal of education was an informed and intelligent citizenry capable of making good choices with respect to the leaders and policies of the nation and the society. They would be informed and thoughtful citizens, conscious members of a public.

This public nature and mission of schools is why they are sites of such contention: They both reflect and shape the collective sense of what we are like—indeed, of who "we" is. There are competing visions of who properly constitutes "we," and the schools are perhaps the primary institutions where the society seeks to both understand and define itself.

Private Education Serves Private Interests

However, although the schools are owned and funded by the public, they are increasingly funded inadequately and un-equally; schools, although nominally public institutions, are increasingly dependent on private and corporate funds, and to that extent, responsive to private desires rather than public needs. This is why the idea of free universal public education was such a radically democratic idea: Schools were to be funded by, and therefore beholden to, the public, not private, interests, whether secular or sectarian.

Many corporations have "adopted" schools, which suggests the dimensions of the problem: Before they can be adopted, schools must first have been abandoned. This funding by pri-vate corporations commits the schools to serve the purposes of the funding institutions rather than the public—those who pay the piper do indeed call the tune. As the attack on "gov-ernment" schools has eroded popular confidence in the sys-tem, powerful individuals and institutions have conducted a well-funded and coordinated effort to transform American education into a completely private system. Private, that is, in the sense of control and goals; these private schools would still be funded with public money funneled to educational corporations through vouchers.

Schooling must be a public enterprise because it is so quintessentially the public enterprise. It is the social institu-tion that exists both to reflect who society is now and its hopes for the future. It is for this reason that, even if all the claims made by advocates of vouchers and private schools about improved test and academic performance were true (they are not!), society should commit itself to improving public schools, not privatizing education.

For the sake of this argument, assume that the claims about the superiority of private education and the effectiveness of voucher programs are true. The public good that education pursues can only be served by the public acting through schools that are shaped by and answer to the public will.

The public good that schools should serve is not the dissemination of personal knowledge or skills important in the marketplace; these are personal and private goods that benefit the individual having the skills and the employer who benefits from trained workers. The public good served by public education is the preparation for democracy that comes with learning to work and play well together, to hear and take into account the needs and interests of the other, to be more than tolerant of those with whom one differs—to be genuinely concerned to understand and accommodate them and their differences, yet still having the ability to make judgments about what behaviors and beliefs must be opposed rather than accommodated.

The point is not that private schools are unable to serve the public good. That would be clearly false; they can and do. The point is more subtle: Any vision of a public good pursued by a private school is, by definition, a private conception of what the public good is. That conception may be one the public would endorse. It may be one and the same as one that the public would develop, but it is significant that the public does not develop it. One problem with privatization is that it means that schools will answer to private interests, not public ones. A second problem is that they create a social fact that inhibits the development of a public; they make the market more robust in the domain where the public should dominate. . . .

Education by Right, Not Permission

One must respond at some point to democracy's requirement for a public; the people cannot be self-governing except as a public made up of mediating publics, joined together in a conversation about common problems and their solutions. Public schools play a vital part in the construction of such a public because they are the institutions in which children are first exposed to democratic life as places where people mix and communicate across differences and seek solutions that take into account the differing needs of different groups and different individuals with different goals and different conceptions of a good life. Public schools, as [educational reformer Deborah] Meier points out, are where children not only come into contact with and learn to deal with difference; public schools are the places where children see adults actually doing democracy, negotiating with each other to find solutions that will accommodate all members to jointly recognized problems. It is the place where individuals engage with people unlike themselves who are there by right, not permission. This is the difference between public and private education. Doing this is the work of democracy; it is what makes democratic life difficult, and it is finessed by a market regime of private education.

*"In the final analysis, the most persua-
sive argument in favor of vouchers is
fundamental fairness."*

Tuition Vouchers Are a Good Alternative to Failing Public Education

Richard Fossey

*Richard Fossey is a professor in the Department of Teacher Edu-
cation and Administration at the University of North Texas. In
the following viewpoint, he refutes objections to school voucher
programs that give parents public money to send their children
to any school of their choice. Fossey claims that vouchers would
not undermine public education but would provide children
trapped in poor school districts with a way to escape a bad education. He also maintains that vouchers would provide disadvantaged parents with strong religious convictions with a way to
send their children to private religious schools.*

As you read, consider the following questions:

1. Where does Fossey believe the public money spent on a
   child attending a public school should go if that child
   leaves that public school?

Richard Fossey, "Who's Afraid of the Big Bad Vouchers?" *UCEA Review*, Winter 2006,
pp. 12–13. Reproduced by permission.

2. If not from vouchers, from what does public education face its most serious competition, according to Fossey?

3. In the author's opinion, how have voucher programs addressed the fear that they would only benefit the privileged to the detriment of the disadvantaged?

In *Zelman v. Harris-Simmons* (2002), the United States Supreme Court repudiated its old hostility to public aid for religious schools, hostility that Justice Clarence Thomas once denounced as being rooted in anti-Catholic nativism. By a five to four vote, the Court upheld the constitutionality of a voucher program for Cleveland school children. The program allows students in Cleveland's crumbling school system to attend private schools at public expense—either secular or religious.

Zelman was universally condemned by public education's major constituency groups—the National School Board Association, the National Parent Teacher Association, the American Association of School Administrators, and the teacher unions. Almost with one voice, these groups denounced the Supreme Court's decision, and several groups vowed to continue fighting vouchers in state legislatures and the courts.

Voucher opponents articulate three major themes. First, vouchers for private schools undermine public education, draining resources away from public schools that are already starved for resources. Second, vouchers for private schools run counter to America's long tradition of democratic education—education that brings children together from all socio-economic, racial, and ethnic backgrounds. Third, private-school vouchers benefit privileged families to the detriment of the disadvantaged—poor children, minority children, and children with disabilities.

The purpose of this essay is to suggest that public education's major constituencies should reconsider their fierce opposition to vouchers. Based on the evidence so far, vouchers do not pose a serious threat to public education or to the democratic ideals it espouses. Moreover, properly constructed voucher programs can provide two important public benefits: 1) they give children in the nation's collapsing inner-city school systems the opportunity to receive a decent education, and 2) they allow families that want religious education for their children the opportunity to obtain it, even if they are too poor to pay private-school tuition.

Vouchers Do Not Significantly Undermine Support for Public Education

First of all, voucher opponents argue that vouchers undermine the public schools. As the National School Board Association (2003) succinctly put it, "[A] dollar spent on a tuition voucher is a dollar drained from a neighborhood public school."

This is true of course, but then shouldn't education dollars go to the institution that educates the child? Cleveland's public schools, for example, lost 75,000 children over a thirty-year period due to a massive outflow of families from the city. No one would argue that the money needed to educate those absent children should stay in Cleveland.

Of course, voucher programs should not be a windfall for private education. Nor should a public school be unduly penalized when a child leaves the public system for a private school. But the notion that education dollars should follow the child seems fair—even when the child leaves a public school for a private one.

More importantly, there is no indication that even a large-scale statewide voucher program—if one were ever enacted—would cripple public education. By and large, Americans are satisfied with their public schools, as the National School Board Association correctly points out. Even if families were given an unrestrained opportunity to participate in a voucher program, it seems doubtful that many would do so.

In fact, when we look at the voucher programs that have appeared so far, most are small initiatives specifically designed to provide better schooling for children in failing schools. The Florida voucher program, for example, adopted by the Florida legislature in 1999, involves only 700 children. The District of Columbia voucher program, established by Congress in 2004, offers private-school scholarships for only 1,700 low-income students. Milwaukee's voucher program, with perhaps 15,000 participants, is the largest municipal voucher initiative; but even that program is small compared to Wisconsin's overall public school enrollment—almost 900,000 students.

If public education faces serious competition, it is from home schooling and charter schools—not vouchers. More than a million children are now home schooled, and public charter schools are strong rivals to traditional public schools in many cities. Dayton, Ohio, has 40 charter schools, which educate about a quarter of the city's students; and 33,000 children are now in charter schools in Detroit.

Vouchers Do Not Undermine the Democratic Values of Public Education

Second, voucher opponents argue that vouchers undermine the democratic values of public education. As the National Education Association put it, "A pure voucher system would only encourage economic, racial, ethnic, and religious stratification in our society. America's success has been built on our ability to unify our diverse populations." This is a strong argument against vouchers, but is it accurate?

In *Democratic Education*, Amy Gutmann, now president of the University of Pennsylvania, wrote the premier defense of American democratic education. In her 1987 book, she argued that democratic education, by which she meant public education, "is an essential welfare good for children as well as the primary means by which citizens can morally educate future citizens." Even Gutmann, however, did not argue that private school options should be eliminated.

Furthermore, Gutmann accurately identified why vouchers have become attractive to so many Americans.

> The appeal of vouchers to many Americans . . . stems, I suspect, from three facts. One is that our public schools, especially in many of our largest cities, are so centralized and bureaucratized that parents, along with other citizens, actually exercise very little democratic control over local schools. The second is that only poor parents lack the option of exiting from public schools, and this seems unfair. The third, and most sweeping fact, is that the condition of many public schools today is bleak by any common-sensical standard of what democratic education ought to be.

It is Gutmann's last point—the bleak condition of many public schools (and here she seems to have been speaking about urban schools)—that is the most critical. In point of fact, most of our inner-city school districts do not reflect democratic values. On the contrary, many of our urban school systems are racially and socioeconomically isolated ghettos with high dropout rates and abysmal records of student achievement where no parent with a reasonable alternative would willingly send a child. It is in these school systems (Cleveland and the District of Columbia are good examples) where vouchers have emerged as a moral alternative and where voucher programs have been largely confined.

Voucher Programs Need Not Discriminate Against the Disadvantaged

Third, voucher opponents maintain that voucher programs benefit the privileged to the detriment of the disadvantaged. Certainly they have that potential. It seems likely, for example, that many private schools would turn away expensive-to-serve children with disabilities if they were allowed to do so. And there is always the potential for race discrimination or favoritism on behalf of the affluent.

The Fallacious "Common Identity" Argument

Public education is vital to creating a common identity as American citizens.

I would find this a slightly more compelling argument if it weren't made mostly by people who live in affluent communities where their fellow citizens are strongly discouraged from moving by zoning and other ordinances that bar the construction of cheap housing. You think some kid growing up in East New York, looking at the crumbling walls as an inexperienced teacher fumbles the lesson plan, thinks to himself "But at least I share a common identity with the kids in Bronxville's public school system whose cars I will someday have the privilege of parking"?

Actually, this makes me think that a lot of the opposition to vouchers is about that affluent suburbanite's need to maintain the delusion that they care about inner-city public schools. Memo to suburban voucher opponents who "support public education": you're already sending your kid to private school. You're just confused because your tuition fees came bundled with granite countertops and hardwood floors.

Megan McArdle, "Vouching for Vouchers,"
The Atlantic.com, Oct 29, 2007.
http://meganmcardle.theatlantic.com.

But these problems can be effectively dealt with if voucher programs are adequately designed. Several of the current voucher programs—Cleveland, for example—are specifically targeted to assist low-income children; and anti-discrimination provisions would seem to be as effective in a voucher program as they are in public education.

Moreover, Catholic schools, which would be major beneficiaries of any large-scale voucher program, have a good record with regard to racial and socioeconomic diversity. [Sociologists James S.] Coleman and [Thomas] Hoffer (1987) concluded that Catholic schools were superior to public schools in educating African Americans, Hispanics, socio-economically disadvantaged children, and children from deficient (single-parent) families. . . .

Fundamental Fairness for the Disadvantaged

In the final analysis, the most persuasive argument in favor of vouchers is fundamental fairness. Affluent families can choose private education for their children—including a religious education—because they can afford to pay for it. Low-income families do not have that choice.

Diane Ravitch, in a 1997 essay, eloquently articulated the unfairness of this state of affairs. "What I argue," Ravitch wrote, "is that it is unjust to compel poor children to attend bad schools. It is unjust to prohibit poor families from sending their children to the school of their choice, even if that school has a religious affiliation. It is unjust to deny free schooling to poor families with strong religious convictions."

Voucher opponents, however sincere, often fail to appreciate the importance that many families attach to religious education. Amy Gutmann, to cite a prominent example, assumes that moral education can take place in a wholly secular atmosphere. Many Americans believe that such a notion is delusional—that a moral foundation is impossible to construct absent religious faith.

In any event, there is profound disagreement about what constitutes moral education in the public schools. Over the years, litigation has broken out between school districts and religious dissenters concerning sex education (*Brown v. Hot, Sexy and Safer Productions, Inc.,* 1995), homosexuality (*Hansen v. Ann Arbor Public Schools,* 2003) and the broader curriculum

(*Altman v. Bedford Central School District*, 2001). As the courts have correctly pointed out, schools cannot be forced to tailor their curriculums to meet the objections of every dissenter—a common curriculum must be taught in the schools (*Brown v. Woodland Joint Unified School District*, 1994; *Brown v. Hot, Sexy and Safer*, 1995). But on the other hand, reasonable alternatives should be available to families with sincere religious objections to what the schools are teaching—and vouchers for religious schools is one such reasonable alternative.

Vouchers Are Not a Threat

In the dawning years of the 21st century, the most serious threat to public education is the abysmal condition of inner-city schools—not vouchers. Alarm about urban education has been the driving force behind much of the voucher activity in the United States. If public education's major constituency groups can dramatically improve the quality of public education for inner-city children, they have nothing to fear from vouchers. And if they cannot achieve this urgent task, then vouchers will be the least of public education's problems.

"Our economic success, our democracy, and our very culture rests solidly on a system of public schools that have been available to all."

Tuition Vouchers Are Not a Good Alternative to Current Public Education

Marcus Egan

Describing the flaws and failures of school voucher programs in Ohio, Wisconsin, and Florida, in the following viewpoint, Marcus Egan claims that the voucher system is demonstrably inferior to public education. He argues that private schools receiving voucher students are not accountable to the public or the government, have often scammed tax dollars from state treasuries, and have not achieved results with voucher students to prove that the voucher system provides any academic benefits. In addition, Egan asserts that the voucher selection process is unfair and undermines the democratic ideals upon which the public education system is built. Marcus Egan is the director of the National School Boards Association's Voucher Strategy Center.

Marcus Egan, *Keeping Public Education Public: Why Vouchers Are a Bad Idea.* Alexandria, VA: National School Boards Association, 2003. Copyright © 2003 by the National School Boards Association. All rights reserved. Reproduced by permission.

As you read, consider the following questions:

1. How are some schools able to reject voucher students who wish to attend them, according to Egan?

2. What are some of the complaints Egan has about the lack of accountability in private schools receiving public voucher money?

3. According to the author, in what ways might private schools not promote the public values supposedly promoted in public schools?

Although the concept of school vouchers has numerous flaws, its central weakness as a public policy is a simple one: Vouchers drain critical dollars from the public schools. Year after year, in proposal after proposal, the public and lawmakers have rejected vouchers because of the negative financial impact vouchers have on public schools. Put simply, a dollar spent on a tuition voucher is a dollar drained from a neighborhood public school. Or, in the case of existing voucher programs, millions of dollars drained from many public schools.

For example, the Milwaukee voucher program, with 11,621 students in the 2002–03 school year, will cost state taxpayers an estimated $65.6 million, and almost half the money (45 percent) will be diverted from the Milwaukee Public Schools and its 105,000 students. While tens of millions of tax dollars have been flowing each year to private schools, the city's public schools have faced multi-million-dollar budget shortfalls that have led to program cuts in recent years. But Milwaukee's public schools are not the only ones to have suffered. During the 2000–01 school year, 237 other school districts lost $2.7 million in state aid and raised local property taxes to help finance the Milwaukee voucher program.

The Cleveland voucher program, which enrolled approximately 5,200 students for the 2002–03 school year, drains more than $11 million a year from the Cleveland Public

Schools. In Cleveland, it's Disadvantaged Pupil Impact Aid that takes the hit—state money that is supposed to pay for preschool, all-day kindergarten, smaller class sizes, and reading improvement programs for disadvantaged public school students.

It's a bitter irony, then, that children already attending private schools have benefited more from vouchers than children in public schools: A recent analysis showed that while 21 percent of students in the program were public school pupils when they applied for a voucher, 33 percent were already attending private schools, and 46 percent were just beginning kindergarten, which means that they, too, might have gone to private school even without a voucher. How can this be? The Cleveland law permits awarding up to half of its vouchers to students currently attending private school. . . .

In addition to taking money away from public schools, voucher legislation is likely to draw the public's attention and energy away from public education and reduce the commitment to working to improve public schools. Relatively few students will get vouchers, but the fanfare surrounding voucher programs may encourage lawmakers—and the public—to believe they have done their bit for school reform. It can give them an excuse to avoid tackling the difficult challenges that continue to face public education, such as raising student achievement, ending the teacher shortage (particularly in high-need schools and subjects), investing in teacher training, helping school boards build and modernize schools, expanding early childhood education programs, and reducing class size. And although robbing public schools to pay for vouchers is a grave injustice to children who are currently in public schools, to the extent that voucher programs distract the public from the need to continue improving public education, these programs also will compromise the education of all children in public schools in years to come.

Vouchers Do Nothing for Most Children

The landmark education bill passed by Congress in 2002 created a slogan that should be a national creed: "No Child Left Behind." Voucher programs, which leave behind scores of children, including those with the greatest needs, will do nothing to help us live by these words.

The push for private school vouchers ignores two significant figures: 47 million and 90 percent. Forty-seven million is the number of children who attend public schools. They represent roughly nine out of every 10 students in the country. From a practical perspective, any serious effort to improve education must start with the public schools, for that is where the overwhelming majority of students are enrolled and will remain. . . .

Voucher Schools Do the Choosing

Although voucher advocates make much of the notion that vouchers will give parents a chance to choose the schools their children attend, it is the private schools that decide whether to accept vouchers, how many students they will admit, and, in some cases, which students they admit.

A public school, as we all know, admits any child from its attendance area if the child comes to the schoolhouse door and requests a seat. It's not that simple with vouchers. Private schools that agree to accept vouchers may limit the number of students they are willing to take. That's up to them. In Cleveland, schools that accept vouchers may use a student's past academic performance in their admissions decisions. In the Milwaukee voucher program, schools that have more applicants than places may hold a lottery to decide which students will be accepted and which ones denied admission. This process, if properly conducted, does give all the applicants an equal chance to use a voucher, but it is a far cry from the American ideal, still embodied by the public schools, of a free education open to every student.

Private schools also might take advantage of interviews with prospective applicants to suggest that a child might not "fit in" and that parents should look elsewhere. Moreover, voucher schools are free to push out or refuse to readmit students they'd like to get rid of. In Milwaukee, the state's official evaluation found an annual attrition rate of 33 percent. The students who left—or were asked to leave—voucher schools were the lower-achieving students. The principal of one voucher school admitted that some students simply were shown the door: "By the end of the second year, it was clear they were not working out, and we let a number go. . . ."

Voucher Programs Can Exclude Children with Disabilities

The neediest children—particularly those with disabilities—often are disproportionately excluded from voucher schools. Schools in two of the nation's most prominent voucher programs, Milwaukee and Cleveland, do not have to educate children with disabilities, including learning disabilities.

Voucher advocates sometimes attempt to obscure this shortcoming. For example, one pro-voucher publication states that "no private school in Milwaukee may exclude any [voucher] eligible student based on specific education needs." The publication fails to mention the fact that voucher schools do not have to offer services to assist students with special needs if it means making anything more than minor adjustments to their programs. The practical result of this policy is that few, if any, children with disabilities will enroll in such schools. . . .

Of course, there is nothing illegal about private schools' excluding special-needs students, because private schools are exempt from many anti-discrimination laws. The Americans with Disabilities Act does not apply to private schools. Section 504 of the Rehabilitation Act of 1973, which prohibits discrimination against the handicapped in education, applies only to programs receiving federal funds. And the nation's special education law, the Individuals with Disabilities Education Act (IDEA), places the responsibility of ensuring an adequate education to students with disabilities on *public*, not private, schools. When all of these factors are combined, it is no surprise that a recent analysis by the RAND Corp. concluded that students with disabilities are under represented in voucher programs.

Vouchers Virtually Eliminate Public Accountability

Americans take for granted that any program they fund with tax money will be accountable to them. Accountability protects taxpayers from having their hard-earned money spent improperly, and it protects the individuals who use the tax-supported program, too. President [George W.] Bush made clear where he stood on the subject of public accountability as he promoted the No Child Left Behind Act: "There are people who are afraid of accountability systems, and, therefore, I become suspicious," he said. "If you're afraid to be held accountable, something must be going wrong. That's how I view it."

President Bush was, of course, talking about public school accountability, but these sentiments should be equally applicable to private schools that accept public money.

But with vouchers, there is no public accountability, because voucher programs channel tax dollars into private schools that need not comply with open-meetings and open-records laws, adhere to state-approved academic standards, or publicly report on students' academic achievement. Thus, taxpayers have no way of discovering how their money is being spent.

Milwaukee voucher schools, for example, face no requirements for teacher certification, curriculum content, student testing, student discipline, enrollment diversity, or compliance with open meetings and open records laws. In Cleveland, voucher schools do not have to meet the state's student testing requirements, and schools with religious affiliations do not even need state accreditation. And in Florida, there are no regulations governing how voucher schools spend tax dollars or how they handle curriculum, student testing, and specialized services for students with disabilities. Nor do Florida's voucher schools have to employ teachers with state certification or even college degrees. It may not be a surprise, then, that Florida has not publicly released the test scores of its voucher students. Despite the fact that the public pays for the voucher program, the state education department has said, "This is not a public-needs-to-know issue. . . ."

Scamming the Public. The loose regulations and lack of public oversight that characterize voucher programs have contributed to instances in which taxpayers have simply been scammed. Two Milwaukee voucher schools inflated their student enrollment numbers to overcharge taxpayers $390,000. Ohio taxpayers were charged $3.5 million in taxicab fees to send children to voucher schools, including nearly half a million dollars in erroneous over-payments for students who were absent or not even enrolled in the schools.

A pair of Cleveland journalists revealed that a city voucher school enrolling 100 students and claiming $268,000 in taxpayer money was not fit to be called a school. The 110-year-old building had no fire alarm or sprinkler system, and it had broken windows, lead paint flaking off the walls at dangerous levels, and little, if any, heat in the winter. Moreover, two-thirds of the school's teachers were unlicensed, including one who had been convicted of first-degree murder for a barroom shooting.

Florida's voucher programs, although relatively new compared to Cleveland's and Milwaukee's, also have had their share of scandals. To give just one example, the state sent $424,000 in tax money to the W. J. Redmond Christian Academy in Palm Beach County despite a laundry list of problems.

Vouchers Are a Double Tax

The main objection to government vouchers is that they are paid for by the taxpayers—the same taxpayers who already fund the public school system. So not only are vouchers an income-transfer program, they amount to a double tax: the taxpayer foots the bill for both public and private schools. Vouchers are "fresh money." Tax money spent on educational vouchers does not come out of tax money spent for traditional schooling. No current voucher proposal even hints at a reduction in funding for public schools to pay for vouchers. To argue that parents who receive vouchers to fund their children's education would merely be getting back some of their own tax dollars is to ignore the fact that most of the parents eligible for vouchers will pay little or no taxes to begin with.

Laurence M. Vance, "The Great Voucher Fraud,"
Freedom Daily, March 25, 2005.www.fff.org.

For one thing, the state had been given five different mailing addresses for the school, including the school owner's home, a motel, and an empty church hall. For another, the state was unable to verify the enrollment of a large number of the voucher students, possibly because as many as a third of them had returned to public schools. A grocery store clerk even complained to the state that the school's principal was trying to cash voucher checks. Parents repeatedly told state officials that the school had no textbooks and that all the children, from kindergartners to twelfth-graders, shared a single classroom. Nevertheless, the state continued to mail out the voucher checks. A spokesperson for the state department of education explained the state's actions with a casual, "We don't ask for an accounting of how the money was spent. . . ."

Vouchers Have Not Raised Academic Achievement

For a number of years after [economist] Milton Friedman first floated his voucher proposal, supporters—and opponents—could only speculate about the effects, if any, of vouchers on student achievement. However, now that we have results from the voucher programs in Milwaukee and Cleveland and a few small programs elsewhere, we are in a position to see that voucher programs have little effect on student achievement.

In 2001, a U.S. General Accounting Office (GAO) report to Congress confirmed that the official evaluations of the Milwaukee and Cleveland voucher programs have "found little or no difference in voucher and public school students' performance." This same GAO review found that some research claiming positive results for vouchers had flaws significant enough to preclude their inclusion in the GAO report.

Kim Metcalf, the researcher who prepared the official state study of the Cleveland voucher program, found that students who attended private schools that were established to take advantage of the voucher program scored lower than their public school peers in all academic subjects. This is particularly significant given the frequent claims that, when vouchers are available, entrepreneurs will be led to create excellent new schools well suited to the needs of the students eligible for vouchers. . . .

Vouchers Undermine the Role of Public Education

Often lost in the debate over vouchers is the important issue of public education's unique and critical role in the success of the United States as a nation. Simply stated, our economic success, our democracy, and our very culture rest solidly on a system of public schools that have been available to all. The fact that the United States has been the democratic and economic leader of the world is perhaps the strongest testament to the success of our public schools—particularly since 90 percent of the nation's students are educated in those schools.

The "common" or public school emerged as the hallmark of American education in the nineteenth century. Horace Mann, who championed the public school as the first state superintendent of Massachusetts, envisioned a system of schools that would be open to all people. His conception took root. Supported by public funds, overseen by state authorities, and open to every child, the common school has become the birthright of every American child.

To ensure that every child can take advantage of this birthright, the nation has a system of public schools funded by tax dollars, and no student can be denied admission on the basis of academic ability, income, race, religion, gender, disability, knowledge of English, or other special need. In addition, state laws and court decisions call for adequacy and equity in educational opportunity in public education, though such goals continue to be a work-in-progress in many locations. Private schools, on the other hand, do not accept all students, and they are not tuition-free.

Promoting Democracy and Common Culture

Public education defines and advances our nation's goals of equity, fairness, and opportunity for all. Public schools strive to ensure that all schoolchildren are prepared for the workplace and that the common values and principles of citizenship needed for a unified nation are taught to all students. While public schools guarantee that the nation's common values are taught, sectarian schools, whose goal is to promote their own beliefs, can make no similar guarantee. Nor can other private schools, which often are devoted to the interests and principles of a particular socioeconomic or ethnic group.

In advancing these democratic goals, public schools clearly belong to the people. The rights of parents, taxpayers, and the public at large to guide public schools are guaranteed through the ballot box, representative school boards, community involvement in public schools, and public accountability.

Among the many shared values taught in public schools is an appreciation of the importance of civil rights. Public schools do not just teach about these rights; they expose students to their application on a personal level so that students learn to exercise, respect, and value them responsibly. But merely teaching about constitutional rights and the protection they afford is not enough. Students need a chance to participate in the application of those rights in institutions that actually extend to them such rights as freedom of religion and expression, equal protection, and due process. Voucher programs, in contrast, take the curious position that the best way to further the values behind public education is to send students to institutions that need not guarantee these basic rights.

"On average, children in single-sex education outperform children of comparative ability in co-ed contexts."

Single-Sex Schools Can Improve Education

Andrew Mullins

Andrew Mullins is the headmaster of Redfield College, a boys school in Sydney, Australia. He believes that single-sex education is advantageous for both boys and girls. In the following viewpoint, Mullins explains that because boys and girls learn in different ways due to physiological differences, they benefit from entirely different educational environments. He states that surveys of test scores support the concept that many children learn better in single-sex classes. Mullins maintains that single-sex education does not inhibit social growth but does require that parents become more involved in rounding out their children's social development.

As you read, consider the following questions:

1. According to a study quoted by Mullins, how does stress affect the learning of girls and boys?
2. How does single-sex schooling meet the special needs of girls, in Mullins's view?

Andrew Mullins, "Single-Sex Schooling," MercatorNet, August 3, 2005. Reproduced by permission.

3. As Mullins writes, how can socializing in school complicate intellectual development for boys and girls?

The comparative benefits of single-sex and coeducational
schooling have been much debated over the past 50 years.
The proponents of single-sex education argue that boys and
girls have differing needs and that their styles of learning are
different. They point to data demonstrating the comparative
under-performance of both boys and girls in co-ed classrooms. Proponents of coeducation argue that mixed education
is more in keeping with the mores of modern Western society,
and that children from co-ed schools are better adjusted. Both
contend that their own approach is truly holistic.

Both Sides of the Debate

The debate has a social component as well. Coeducation is
sometimes regarded as a solution to the failure of the modern
family to provide sufficiently for the effective socialization and
moral development of children. The financial savings of using
shared facilities have led governments to amalgamate formerly
single-sex schools and open new co-ed schools, both public
and private. In some countries governments have told independent schools to embrace coeducation or forfeit public
funding.

A new element in the debate is widespread agreement that
somehow education is failing boys. Boys are generally outperformed by girls; statistics of self harm and depression amongst
boys are alarming; there seems to be a growing alienation of
boys from their parents and fathers in particular. Psychologists
write of the "father hunger" of boys who grow up without
sufficient input from their natural father.

As Western society strives for gender equality, everyone
has become more alert to the unfairness of discrimination on
the basis of sex. This argument is used by both sides. Proponents of single-sex education argue that only through single-

sex education are the specific needs of boys and girls met. Proponents of coeducation argue that coeducation ensures equity of access to educational facilities and courses. Single-sex education supporters reply that equality of the sexes does not necessitate identical provision for males and females, and that the best way of attending to the needs of boys and girls is to offer them facilities and courses that satisfy their unique requirements.

Boys and Girls Are Wired to Learn in Different Ways

It seems beyond dispute that boys and girls learn at different paces and in different ways. This is not a matter of gender bias, but of experience verified time and again by psychological research. The view from the 1970s that gender traits are mere cultural constructs has been discredited. Cross-cultural studies over the past 30 years reveal that gender differences across the wide variety of cultures are remarkably constant.

Here are some relevant differences. According to a 2001 study, women use the right and left hemispheres of the brain to process language; men use only the left hemisphere. In general men are more likely to use one area of the brain for a given activity; women are more likely to use more of the brain. Studies show that women respond to directions that include data about what they will see and hear; men prefer abstract directions. Girls' brains develop through adolescence so that girls are better able to discuss their feelings; boys' brains do not. Research is revealing major physiological differences in the brains of even pre-adolescent boys and girls. For example, seven-year-old girls hear better than boys.

These physical differences lead to differences in the way boys and girls learn. Teachers need to encourage girls, while boys need a reality check. Direct challenging works well with boys and they tend to respond to clear boundaries. Emotional activity is processed in a completely different part of the brain in older girls compared with older boys. It has been suggested that girls respond more innately to literature and that they more easily make links between ideas and emotions. In stories, girls tend to respond to nuances of character, boys to action. Role-playing exercises allowing a student to explore character work particularly well for girls. Inductive exercises allowing girls to act hypothetically also work well. There is evidence that boys respond more to structured lessons, finite tasks, and perhaps to the more abstract. Girls tend to respond more readily to group work and team work. One fascinating study suggests that under certain circumstances stress has a beneficial effect on male learning, but that it can impair the learning of a female, and that this characteristic is wired in the male brain from before birth.

Most Children Learn Better in a Single-Sex Environment

On average, children in single-sex education outperform children of comparative ability in co-ed contexts. In a 20-year Australian study of 270,000 students, Ken Rowe found that both boys and girls performed between 15 and 22 percentile points higher on standardised tests when they attended single-sex schools. The National Foundation for Educational Research in England found that, even after controlling for student ability and other background factors, boys and girls performed significantly better academically in single-sex schools than in co-ed schools. Students in Jamaica attending single-sex schools outperformed students in co-ed schools in almost every subject tested. A 1997 study by Jean and Geoffrey Underwood showed that girl-girl pairings performed best on tasks, and that girl-boy pairings tended to depress the achievement of the girls involved.

Boys and girls experience the benefits of schooling in different ways. British studies suggest that females more than males benefit academically from single-sex education: they participate more in class, develop higher self esteem, score higher in aptitude tests, are more likely to choose sciences and other male domains at tertiary level, and are more successful in careers. Research suggests that boys dominate the classroom in a co-ed environment. Boys can behave more loudly. Some research has shown that girls receive fewer encouraging comments than boys in co-ed environments. Studies by Cornelius Riordan suggest that children from underprivileged backgrounds are the greatest beneficiaries of single-sex schooling. The message of all this research is simple: there are no differences in what girls and boys can learn, but here are big differences in the best way to teach them.

Single-Sex Education Meets the Needs of Boys Better

Boys and girls have different needs, and education which respects personal differences must take this into account. On a practical level, the intuitively directed and affectively oriented styles of learning which suit most girls are not always compatible with the more structured and practical approaches which appeal to boys. Single-sex schooling allows teachers to tailor their teaching style to the boys and facilitates a more rounded educational experience. In a co-ed school, boys can opt out of curriculum areas where they would be outperformed.

Furthermore, there is evidence that mixed classrooms can discriminate against either boys or girls depending on the subject, the gender of the teacher, the teacher's methodologies, and the prevailing culture in the school. Some schools have now started running single-sex classrooms in English and other humanities subjects to improve the performance of boys. The pilot study that demonstrated improved performance of boys in this context has been known as the Cotswold Experiment.

Single-Sex Education Meets the Needs of Girls Better

Single-sex education has clear benefits for girls. In the first place, it often gives them expanded educational opportunities by allowing them to pursue non-traditional disciplines for girls, such as mathematics or science. Single-sex schooling also offers more opportunities to girls to exercise leadership. When girls and boys are in the same classroom, the boys tend to dominate and overshadow equally talented girls.

On an emotional level, single-sex education puts less pressure on girls, especially in adolescence. At that age, girls are more prone than boys to suffer from low self esteem. It is difficult to manage this issue in a co-ed climate when boys dominate in the classroom and when they receive more recognition, allowance for misbehaviour and encouragement.

Single-Sex Education Makes Greater Provision for Gender Role Modeling

The shortage of male teachers in the primary classroom is a concern in many countries. In the first six years of school, many boys in co-ed schools seldom encounter a male teacher. Because children imitate those they admire, it is common sense to ensure that boys and girls find in their teachers truly admirable role models. The example of professionalism, values and consistently positive behaviour is most important. But there are other aspects of example that are gender-specific. A boy learns what it means to be a man from his father, but this is reinforced if there are other admirable men in his life. This is also true for girls and their female teachers.

Single-Sex Schooling Allows Boys and Girls to Mature at Their Own Pace

Girls mature earlier than boys: they are better behaved, more diligent and more sensible and they find it easier to relate to the adult world. For all these reasons, it is often argued that girls exert a civilising influence on boys. Whilst this may be true in some situations, the converse is also true: boys can un-civilise girls. When adolescent girls and boys study together, there is much evidence that a proportion will end up distracted from their work.

Single-sex schooling is often criticised for reinforcing negative images of masculinity. Unfortunately this can even happen in co-ed schools. The problem is not solved by bringing girls and boys together, but by vigilantly managing the culture in a school and sub-groups in the school.

Single-Sex Schooling Does Not Handicap Children Socially

There is no evidence that children who have attended co-ed schools enter adult relationships that are more stable or fulfilling with the opposite sex. Assertions that children from co-ed backgrounds are better prepared for adult life seem to be flawed. There is a higher rate of unplanned pregnancies (and by implication, of terminated pregnancies) for girls in co-ed schools. One study has shown that students from single-sex schooling are not noticeably thwarted in the development of relationships with the opposite sex either at school or later at university.

Coeducation can allow socialising to complicate intellectual development. Of course a positive school culture and the superior training of teachers can work against this. But it is difficult to protect impressionable young people from the images of precocious intimacy that saturate the media. Since emotional attraction and physical attraction works first of all at the level of physical proximity, there seems a strong argument to separate a teenager's academic world from his or her social world. In a coeducational secondary classroom the lines between social life and school can become blurred. Single-sex education allows children to think about things "other than their hormones."

Test Scores and Discipline Improve

Seattle's Thurgood Marshall Elementary School used to be a failing school in one of that city's poorest neighborhoods. Then the school's energetic principal, Benjamin Wright, reinvented the school as a dual academy: girls in all-girls classrooms, boys in all-boys classrooms. The results have been encouraging. Boys' test scores on the reading portion of the Washington Assessment of Student Learning, or WASL, exam have increased from the 10th percentile to the 66th percentile. Girls have benefited as well. In the year before the change, when the school was co-ed, not a single girl passed the math portion of the WASL. In the year after the change, 53 percent of the girls passed. And the improvement has not been limited to grades and test scores: Student behavior has also improved. Discipline referrals dropped from 30 referrals per day to fewer than two a day—"overnight," according to Mr. Wright.

Leonard Sax,
Education Week, March 2, 2005.

Single-Sex Schooling Makes It Easier to Be a Good Parent

Single-sex schools also provide parents with an opportunity to manage more effectively the social development of their children, particularly in the early years. It makes it easier for them to impart education about sexual matters in a way consistent with their values. Of course when parents choose to send their children to single-sex schools they will need to have much more initiative in providing for the social development of their children. They should set up many opportunities for boys to mix with girls in a family setting during childhood, well before they turn 14 or 15. It is very late to be starting to talk with a child about these issues once he or she has reached mid secondary school.

An undeniable problem for all families is the gulf between home life and a teenager's social world. Children must feel they can bring their friends home. Coeducational schooling does little to help because it creates a social environment which is totally beyond the parents' knowledge and largely outside their control. Unhappily when youth culture becomes divorced from family life, a certain percentage of children are sure to end up badly damaged.

Even if single-sex schooling is better for children, it demands more of their parents because they have to take responsibility for helping their children acquire mature social skills. It is easier for parents who send their children to co-ed schools to shirk this responsibility, even though this is not a task which can be delegated to anyone else. Indeed, the notion that parents can wash their hands of the problems of teenage social life may account for some of the popularity of co-ed education. But although relinquishing their leadership role might make parents' lives easier, the children often suffer from their neglect.

> *"The assumption that separate schools for boys and girls will make schools and districts better for students is way off the mark."*

Single-Sex Schools Will Not Improve Education

Elena Silva

Elena Silva is a senior policy analyst at Education Sector, an independent think tank in Washington, DC. In the following viewpoint, Silva contends that single-sex schools are catering to a growing trend in America to favor choice in education. Silva believes that this desire for choice may involve important sacrifices, however. She claims that that there is no clear evidence that gender segregation benefits learning, and in her view, any positive outcomes from such separation might be attributable to better teachers or more interested students. Finally, Silva fears that same-sex classrooms run counter to the notion of gender equality and may resurrect old gender biases that many have fought so long to overcome.

As you read, consider the following questions:

1. What does Silva say "we know about teaching and learning" that same-sex education seems to ignore?

Elena Silva, "Boys and Girls Are More Alike in School Than They Are Different," DelawareOnline.com, March 26, 2008. Reproduced by permission.

2. According to the author, what two student groups have been largely overlooked in research about the value of single-sex education?

3. Why have many single-sex schools turned back to coed classrooms, as Silva states?

Prestige Academy is hoping to open [in] fall [2008] in Wilmington [Delaware] as an all-boys public charter school. Its mission is a worthy one: to serve low-income black and Latino boys, a population that tests below average on nearly every measure of school achievement.

As a part of a growing movement toward single-sex education, the school has created a stir in the Legislature, which has been debating the fate of Prestige since [2007].

Debates like these, premised on whether state law should allow gender separation in public schools, are increasingly common across the country as a solution for failing schools and struggling students. The move toward single-sex education has been propelled by recent changes to Title IX, the federal law prohibiting gender discrimination in education.

A Change to Title IX

It's the gender equivalent of *Brown v. Board of Education*. Title IX was designed to ensure that schools educate boys and girls equally and together, with few exceptions.

But in 2006 the U.S. Department of Education lifted the restrictions on single-sex education. Since then, all-boy and all-girl schools and classes have been cropping up all over the country. A recent article in the *New York Times* magazine reported that the number of single-gender public schools has grown from just two in 1995 to 49 [in 2008].

The number of public schools experimenting with single-sex classes is now reported to be more than 350.

The change to Title IX and resultant surge in single-sex public schooling is not surprising given the movement toward more choice in public education. The belief that parents deserve more publicly funded options for their children's education is stronger than ever. And in poor urban districts with failing schools, fresh educational alternatives for children are difficult, even foolish, to pass up.

Single-gender schools seem logical, then, to a public that accepts that gender differences are real and likes the idea of expanding choices.

Equivocal Evidence

But the link between gender and learning is weak. And the assumption that separate schools for boys and girls will make schools and districts better for students is way off the mark.

The current push for single-gender public schools rests on the claim that boys and girls have different educational needs. This ignores what we know about teaching and learning—that individual children learn differently and that more of such differences are found within one gender than between boys and girls.

These facts are confirmed by research here in the United States and abroad. There's no conclusive evidence that single-sex education results in better learning outcomes.

Even the U.S. Department of Education, in its own review of 44 research studies on single-sex education, acknowledges that the results are "equivocal" and steered clear from a patent endorsement of single-sex schools.

The vast majority of single-sex research, including the studies used for the U.S. Department of Education's review, has focused on Catholic and all-girl schools. Some of these studies show improvement in girls' self-esteem and some academic measures.

Very few studies have focused on boys or poor and minority students. One study by researcher Cornelious Riordan found that poor and minority students performed better academically in single-sex schools. However, Riordan acknowledges these students likely did better because single-sex schools have a greater academic orientation and focused curriculum.

Since the majority of single-sex alternatives serve smaller numbers of students, provide more individual attention and emphasize academic instruction, claiming gender as the cause for higher achievement seems spurious.

Separate Is Not Always Equal

Black and Latino males are in dire need of targeted intervention—and educators and reformers must not turn away from this problem. But we should be cautious about crediting gender for the success of quality schooling, especially given the pitfalls of designing a gender-based education system.

Touting single-sex education as yet another alternative for students downplays the potential negative effects of segregated schooling. The core lesson—that separate is not always equal—is one that proponents must bear in mind.

While the original Title IX might be viewed as overly rigid, restraining choice and opportunity, a flood of single-sex schools and classrooms could revive old patterns of gender bias and discrimination and engender new ones. Gender-based teaching, rather than broadening learning for students, has the potential to narrow it into girl- and boy-specific boxes.

Moreover, the new regulations call for "substantially equal" opportunities for both sexes. But the meaning of "equal" and how it will be ensured remains undefined.

Unfriendly Reactions to Same-Sex Schools

Costly lawsuits are nearly certain as a result. Livingston Parish, a Louisiana district just outside Baton Rouge, dropped its plan to pilot a single-sex school in August 2006 after it was sued by the American Civil Liberties Union for gender discrimination.

Districts and schools considering single-sex education should be wary of other practical barriers. Although the new regulations allow for substantially mere flexibility in offering

Undermining the Evidence That Gender Segregation Improves Academic Achievement

Although supporters of single-sex schools cite social science research in support of their position, properly evaluated, these studies indicate that certain characteristics often present in a single-sex setting—such as small classrooms, extensive resources, well-trained teachers, and advanced educational methods—are in fact the basis for any positive outcomes that may be found. The single-sex factor is not dispositive, and the causative characteristics could be equally available in a coeducational setting. Recent data suggest that once these other variables are controlled for, measurable differences between students' performance in single-sex and coeducational programs disappear.

American Civil Liberties Union, Single-Sex Notice of Intent Comments to the Department of Education, July 8, 2002.

single-sex options, the law still holds that schools must be voluntary for students and offer a comparable class or school for all other students.

While individual charter schools would be exempt from these criteria, the district must still provide substantially equal classes at another school within the district. In practical terms, districts would conceivably need twice as many schools to provide same-sex options to both genders or a comparable co-ed option.

For schools, single-sex options would mean many more teachers (and classrooms) and a potential nightmare in scheduling. Many districts have reluctantly turned away from single-sex options, or switched back to co-ed models, because of these logistical and budget challenges.

The Necessary Elements of a Successful School

With no clear evidence that single-sex schools provide a better education for children, and a host of challenges to implementing them well, designing schools around gender is little more than a distraction from what failing schools—and the kids they serve—need.

The leaders of Prestige Academy seem to understand the essentials of a quality school and have set their sights on providing these: skilled and effective teachers and leaders, high academic standards, and strong support inside the school and in the community to meet these standards. The school is likely to succeed, not because it is limited to boys but because it is organized around these elements of quality education.

To be sure, girls will seek this same quality. To that end, Delaware legislation includes the condition that a "substantially equal" all-girls school will be also approved within two years.

If a girls school doesn't materialize, there is no stated penalty. But the state should be prepared all the same for legitimate lawsuits arguing that separate is not equal.

Periodical Bibliography

The following articles have been selected to supplement the diverse views presented in this chapter.

Steve Adcock	"Our Nation's Future Depends on School Choice," SmallGovTimes.com, March 30, 2007. www.smallgovtimes.com.
Glenn Cook	"School Voucher Battle Heats Up Again," *American School Board Journal*, October 2007.
Matthew Davidson and Thomas Lickona	"Smart & Good," *Independent School*, Winter 2007.
Denis P. Doyle	"Why Markets Are Important (And What They Could Do for Public Education)," *Education Week*, January 16, 2008.
Denis P. Doyle	"Pro-Choice," June 9, 2007.
Economist	"Free to Choose and Learn," May 5, 2007.
David Gelernter	"A World Without Public Schools," *Weekly Standard*, June 4, 2007.
Charles L. Glenn	"The Wrong Debate," *Education Week*, November 29, 2006.
Carrie Kilman	"One Nation, Many Gods," *Education Digest*, November 2007.
Jeremy Leaming	"Vouchers Vanquished," *Church & State*, December 2007.
Michele McNeil	"A Choice Showdown," *Education Week*, October 24, 2007.
Zachary M. Seward	"Long-Delayed Education Study Casts Doubt on Value of Vouchers," *Wall Street Journal*, July 15, 2006.
Rona Wilensky	"For Some High-School Students, Going to College Isn't the Answer," *Chronicle of Higher Education*, April 27, 2007.

Should Religious and Moral Values Be Taught as Part of Public Education?

Chapter Preface

Although the last half of the twentieth century witnessed several court cases in which the practice or expression of religion had been banned from public schools, the issue does not seem to have lost any of its contentiousness in the twenty-first century. Many Americans see the involvement of the courts as government effectively limiting the First Amendment right to freedom of religious expression. Others view the separation as the result of an ongoing liberal campaign to purge God from sacred American institutions that were created by religious men who fully understood that God's law and human law were intertwined. Even a 2006 Pew Research Center survey found that 69 percent of Americans agree with the notion that "liberals have gone too far in trying to keep religion out of the schools and the government."

The American Civil Liberties Union (ACLU) and other civil liberties advocates do not share that view. While tolerant of individual, nondisruptive student prayer, for example, the ACLU asserts that any attempt by a public school administrator or representative to lead a school-wide prayer would violate the civil liberties of students and faculty. Similarly, students could learn about Hinduism in school but could not be led in a Hindu prayer. "Students may be taught about religion, but public schools may not teach religion," the ACLU maintains. However, the same Pew survey that found Americans less worried about keeping religion out of government and schools also showed that 58 percent of Americans favor the teaching of biblical creationism alongside evolution in the classroom.

Primarily in smaller townships, school boards have revised science curricula to instate the teaching of creationism or intelligent design in addition to evolutionary theories. In November 2004, for example, the school board in the city of

Grantsburg, Wisconsin, added creationism to its science classes amidst widespread uproar from academics and concerned organizations. In 2005 President George W. Bush spoke in favor of schools teaching intelligent design as an alternative to Darwinism, though he added that the choice is one left to school boards and not one that should be handed down by the federal government. Critics still denounce the teaching of these alternatives because they claim there is no scientific evidence to support the claims of intelligent design or other such theories.

In the following chapter, proponents and adversaries debate the merit of teaching religious values and theories in public education. Some assert that religion should be an object of study and not indoctrination. Others contend that prizing evolution over alternative concepts is limiting the free range of ideas that should be part of education. Finally, some worry that by excluding a moral education from public schools, educators will be depriving students of important tools needed to become good citizens and good Americans.

> "We need citizens who have the strength
> of character to uphold democratic free-
> dom in the face of unprecedented chal-
> lenges at home and abroad."

Character Education
Should Be Part of
the American School System

Charles C. Haynes and Marvin W. Berkowitz

*In the following viewpoint, Charles C. Haynes and Marvin W.
Berkowitz claim that the American education system is too focused on academic achievement and is allowing character-
building to fall out of school curriculum. In the authors' view,
instilling pride and self-esteem in young people has valuable
civic rewards and would help to correct class absenteeism, lack of
motivation, and even poor moral character. Haynes and Berkowitz are hopeful, though, that a resurgent interest in moral education will convince school administration to reinvigorate this
once-prized part of the learning process. Charles C. Haynes is a
scholar at the First Amendment Center in Washington, DC.
Marvin W. Berkowitz is a professor of character education at the
University of Missouri in St. Louis.*

Charles C. Haynes and Marvin W. Berkowitz, "What Can Schools Do?" *USA Today*,
February 20, 2007. Reproduced by permission of the authors.

As you read, consider the following questions:

1. Who said, "To educate a person in mind and not morals is to educate a menace to society"?

2. What are some of the "teachable moments" Haynes and Berkowitz mention in the viewpoint?

3. According to the authors, what kinds of problems does researcher Victor Battistich claim character education can prevent?

After the endless headlines involving corrupt politicians, corporate cheats, doped-up sports stars and Internet predators, you might think that the American people would be demanding more character education in schools.

Think again.

"Good character," like the weather, gets a lot of talk—but too little action. We bemoan the loss of integrity and lack of responsibility in American public life. We decry the numbing statistics about teenage substance abuse, sexual promiscuity and gang activity. We wring our hands over surveys that report widespread cheating in schools and colleges. And then we move on to more important things.

Test scores, for example.

That's right: Standardized test results seem to trump everything else in education these days. No matter how many warning bells are sounded about the crisis of character in our society and despite the long-standing understanding that education is for the whole child, all we want to hear is how each school did on the exam.

A Character-Building Success Story

Reading and math are important, but if we care about our kids (and our future) shouldn't we be paying more attention to the kinds of human beings who do the math and read the books?

"To educate a person in mind and not in morals," said Theodore Roosevelt, "is to educate a menace to society."

Fortunately, taking academics and character seriously in schools isn't an either/or proposition. Done well, character development enhances academic performance. Just ask Kristen Pelster, principal of Ridgewood Middle School, a rural/suburban school of about 503 students (42% of them economically disadvantaged) in Arnold, Mo.

When Pelster arrived as assistant principal six years ago, Ridgewood had all the marks of the proverbial "failing school": high absenteeism, low academic achievement and a constant stream of discipline problems. Located in a poor community plagued by inadequate housing and meth labs, the school had graffiti on the walls, profanity echoing in the halls and a rusty chain fence surrounding it. It could have been the movie set for *Blackboard Jungle*.

Working as a team, Pelster and then-principal Tim Crutchley, who was also new, made a commitment to transform Ridgewood. First, they diagnosed the problem: Students didn't feel as though anyone cared about them or the school.

Then they articulated a vision for "a school where there is caring, a sense of belonging and academic achievement."

Facing angry parents and a dispirited staff, Crutchley and Pelster knew they had much convincing to do. When they first arrived at Ridgewood, dozens of parents had requested that their children be moved to another school. Step One was to clean up the physical environment. (The rusty fence was the first thing to go.)

Initially, "caring" was a lot like "tough love." Crutchley and Pelster raised the bar on attendance, often going to truant students' homes to bring them to school. They established a "failure is not an option" program that prohibited the giving of zeros for missing work. Students had to make up missing homework during lunch hour. Teachers were required to integrate character education into academic lessons and behavior management.

By the end of the first year, the two leaders had won over a core team of teachers, critical support that, with the help of parents and members of the community, let the school progress.

Getting Students and Faculty Involved

The Ridgewood activists learned early on that "character education" is far more than slogans or quick-fix lessons about a word of the week. To be effective, character education must become integral to the daily actions of everyone in the school community.

It starts with the faculty. Early in the process, Crutchley and Pelster drove out teachers who didn't show concern for students and recruited teachers who did.

They allocated resources to provide staff development. This modest investment in teacher training—a few thousand dollars—constituted almost the entire cost to implement their plan.

Effective character education is not an add-on, but instead uses "teachable moments" in every classroom. Seventh-grade teacher Kacie Heiken, for example, has her students write and illustrate fairy tales that have a positive moral lesson. The students go to elementary schools and read their stories to classes before donating the books to a local children's hospital.

In American history classes, students study veterans, war and military service, culminating in a school-wide celebration of Veterans Day that includes breakfast and a patriotic slide show for local veterans and their families.

Science students recently collaborated with a local church group to build a nature trail.

Ridgewood's effort extends beyond the curriculum. For half an hour each day, students meet with an adult mentor in

Integrating Character Education into the Elementary School Classroom

After considering my students' needs, my weekly schedule, the standard first-grade curriculum areas, and the ideas in [Timothy G. Rusnak's] *An Integrated Approach to Character Education*, I realized that I could integrate character education into what I was already teaching. Many stories in children's literature, for example, reflect lessons in morals and virtues; we can read and discuss these moral lessons without taking time from core subjects. Character education also fits well with social studies and health topics. Accepting individual differences, showing courage, developing citizenship, taking responsibility for oneself, and making positive choices were already part of my first-grade materials, so the hurdle of finding time for character education became less intimidating. I needed only to shift the focus of my teaching to emphasize the themes of character.

Gloria Rambow Singh, Educational Leadership, October 2001.

small family-like advisory groups. "The advisory helps form strong relationships between staff and student and among students. It creates a sense of being more of a family than an institution," Crutchley says.

But character education at Ridgewood isn't solely, or even predominantly, a top-down process. Daily class meetings include ethics discussions led by students. A one-semester course in "teen leadership" prepares students to take the lead in implementing an honor code and dealing with problems such as bullying.

Parents also play a key role. After all, they have primary responsibility for the moral development of their kids. While some parents have abdicated this responsibility, most want schools to reinforce and model the moral values taught at home. Many Ridgewood parents now volunteer at the school, and attendance at parent conferences has risen from 44.5% in 2000 to 75% in 2005.

The Results Prove Character Education Works

Today, Crutchley is assistant superintendent of the district and Pelster, now principal, presides over a transformed Ridgewood.

Academic performance is up, disciplinary referrals are down by more than 70%, and the student failure rate has dropped to zero. Attendance has also improved, with the formerly daily home visits for truant students now down to four or five per year.

The rusty fence and graffiti are long gone, replaced by displays of student classwork and high expectations: Ridgewood has been on Missouri's list of Top Ten Most Improved Schools for four of the past five years.

In October, Ridgewood was one of 10 schools and districts in the nation to be recognized as a 2006 National School of Character by the Character Education Partnership.

Ridgewood's turnaround may be unusual, but it is not unique. "Schools of Character," schools that are implementing a comprehensive plan for character education, can be found in school districts across the USA. No study has yet been done on how many schools are providing character education, but the need is clear and the interest is understandably immense.

Ridgewood is a remarkable case study, but the success of character education is well-documented. It works.

Victor Battistich of the University of Missouri-St. Louis, examined all the scientific research of the past 15 years and concluded that "comprehensive, high-quality character education" can prevent a wide range of problems, including "aggressive and antisocial behaviors, drug use, precocious sexual activity, criminal activities, academic underachievement and school failure."

An Idea That Is Making a Comeback

So why aren't all schools doing it? In the early history of public education, developing good character was seen as an essential part of preparing people for citizenship in a democratic society. But in the latter part of the 20th century, many public schools moved away from the traditional emphasis on character and citizenship as American society grew more complex and diverse.

Today, character education is making a comeback. Thirty-one states mandate or encourage character education by statute. While pronouncements by legislatures don't necessarily translate into quality character education programs, it's a start.

Much is at stake in getting this right. At this critical moment in America's history, we need far more than higher math and reading scores. We need citizens who have the strength of character to uphold democratic freedom in the face of unprecedented challenges at home and abroad.

"Only a virtuous people are capable of freedom," is the familiar aphorism from Benjamin Franklin. Less well-known, but worth recalling, is the warning in the sentence that follows: "As nations become corrupt and vicious, they have more need of masters."

> *"Many people who create character pro-*
> *grams surely do so out of sincere con-*
> *cern and desire to help make a better*
> *world. But when their programs present*
> *complex and multifaceted virtues as if*
> *they were simple and easy, they do a*
> *great disservice."*

Character Education Is the Wrong Way to Teach Values

Bobby Ann Starnes

Bobby Ann Starnes is a former teacher and cofounder of Full Circle Curriculum and Materials, a nonprofit organization that provides support to educators in Montana. In the following viewpoint, Starnes discusses how confused she was when her grade school adopted a character education program. Believing that character virtues are taught by example, Starnes says she was unsure how to teach values that she knew were complex and could not be reduced to simple words or slogans. She argues that trying to make values simplistic for students is condescending and does not allow children to think about how different people may define specific value traits such as truth, integrity, and justice.

Bobby Ann Starnes, "Don't 'Dumb Down' Character Education," *Education Digest*, September 2006, pp. 39–43. Reproduced by permission.

As you read, consider the following questions:

1. Why does Starnes believe her mother's patriotic songs were a better instructive source of values than character education programs?

2. Why did Starnes find it objectionable to reward students with paper citations for doing "worthy" acts?

3. What does Starnes fear that character education programs are really about?

In June, I traveled to eastern Kentucky to attend a conference on community sustainability, an important challenge for the small communities snuggled into the state's narrow valleys and along its rugged mountainsides. In these places, like so many other communities across the nation, children are regularly educated to believe that rich, full, and successful lives can be lived only if they leave their communities and their cultures far behind.

Going to eastern Kentucky is always a pleasure for me. It is home and a place I do not visit often enough. When I do, my mind is always flooded with childhood memories. As I prepared for this trip and what I would say in my little speech, my mind returned to the hundreds of trips my family made from Dayton, Ohio, where my parents moved when mechanization replaced my father's pick and shovel in eastern Kentucky's coal-mining industry.

We lived in Ohio, but it was never home. Home was the narrow sliver of bottom land running alongside Caney Creek in Knott County, where the first Owens family member settled just after the Revolutionary War and where generations of Owenses after him eked out a living on the rocky hillsides that rise sharply on both sides of the creek.

Anxious to Escape

Going home was for many years the central focus of our family life. As soon as my father got off work on Friday night, our family would pile into our ancient Buick and head south along Route 25, or what was then called the Hillbilly Highway. The traffic was always backed up from Cleveland to Cincinnati, jammed with other families like ours, anxious to escape lives in the often-hostile cities and find peace among our extended families.

From time to time, the old Buick actually made the trip without breaking down. On those occasions, it was about a 12-hour drive. And that was with no video players, no hand-held games, and no iPods to keep a car full of kids amused. But that didn't matter, because my mother loved to sing.

With the glow of passing headlights casting shadows that seemed to reveal monsters spying on us at every turn, my father drove the dark and narrow roads that would lead us to my aunt's front porch somewhere near the break of dawn. And as he drove, my brothers and sisters and I drifted in and out of a fuzzy sleep, and my mother serenaded us with what my younger brother and I later came to call "the concert of death, doom, and sorrow."

Carrying a tune was not among my mother's talents. But that wasn't important. To her, it was all about the lyrics.

Her songs recounted horrific traffic and mining accidents, tragic deaths of loved ones, and sorrowful laments of the wrongfully incarcerated, peppered with stories of bravery and patriotism, sacrifice and sin, tragedy and heartbreak.

Among her favorites were the World War II songs. She particularly loved one about Johnny, a young man with a rather weak educational history whom the kids always taunted on test day by singing, "Johnny got a zero, he got another zero."

As the story unfolds, we learn that Johnny is now a fighter pilot particularly adept at shooting down Japanese planes called Zeroes. Thus, the refrain that my mother sang, seeming always to fight back tears: "Johnny got a Zero, he got another Zero." She was always a sap for such irony.

Another favorite recounted the tale of a young mountain boy begging an Army recruiter to let him join up. "Though I realize I'm crippled, that is true, sir," he explains. "Please don't judge my courage by my twisted knee."

The Source of Values

My mother always got particularly riled up when she sang the refrain, "God gave me the right to be a free American, and for that precious right I would gladly die. There's a Star Spangled Banner waving somewhere. In that heaven there must be a place for me."

Her emotion may have grown out of the death of her younger brother, Robert—for whom I was named—who was killed on the beaches of Normandy. But to me it was always about doing right and sacrificing for the greater good.

These were the songs of my childhood—no purple dinosaur singing songs about friendship, no trips to Mr. Rogers' Neighborhood, no moralistic lectures from Captain Kangaroo or Mr. Green Jeans, just blood and guts, death and despair.

Years later, my brother and I laughed about what we figured was our mother's version of nursery rhymes. But we also thought that the songs did more to help us form our values than all those years of opening each school day with the Pledge of Allegiance.

That leads me to a concept that, frankly, I just don't understand—character education. I think I understand the notion of "character," and I'm pretty sure that I have a handle on the meaning of "education." Trouble for me arises when those two words sit side by side. Together, they seem to form a concept that leaves me . . . well . . . puzzled.

One year I taught in a school that had adopted a "character program." Although my days were filled with more obligations and responsibilities than even a superhuman could have met, I was expected to teach my students character, not through my actions or interactions or through purposeful reflective thought, not in the normal course of daily events, but with a kit.

Slogans and Puppets

So you might think that, since I *taught* character education, I would know what it is. Sadly, the opposite is true. My experience with character education left me flustered and confused.

Things seemed pretty clear at first. The full-service character education program my school purchased provided me with a huge box filled with flash cards, vocabulary lists, posters, puppets, CDs, lesson plans, and more.

Its driving force was a weekly character word. One week, it was pride, another it was helpful, or responsibility, or promptness, and so on, week after week after week. Each lesson plan included a little moral—or moralistic—vignette, suggestions for role playing, writing prompts, and little mottoes and slogans the kids were to memorize and parrot back in response to some canned question I was to pose.

Judging Worthiness

Another important job I was also assigned was "catching" children doing something right and rewarding them with a piece of paper proclaiming their worthiness. This was not as easy as it sounded, since kids seemed to do a lot of things right, and I couldn't figure out how I could possibly reward them each time I "caught" them or how I could keep track of all the little slivers of paper they would collect. That alone seemed like a full-time job to me.

About once a month, we gathered for a little assembly during which the assistant principal gave the kids a pep talk about one virtue or another and then read the names of students who had been caught doing things right. Usually the "right things" consisted of such acts as "Johnny opened the door for the teacher when her hands were full," "Mary picked up the trash from around her desk," "Bill shared his crayons."

I began to wonder what kind of kids populated our school. If opening a door for a teacher whose hands were full merited special recognition in an assembly, what kinds of behavior were the kids who *didn't* get recognition engaging in? Were they blocking the door? Taunting the teacher about being unable to get into the building? Throwing rocks at her or something else so ugly that I couldn't even imagine it?

My kids certainly seemed polite, kind, and helpful. But apparently, evil children lurked in our school hallways. Over time, though, I began to notice that such virtuous behaviors were most often performed by children in the special education programs. This was exceedingly disturbing to me, but someone explained that they "never win anything, so this is something they can win." It didn't seem right to me. Could this be a character flaw in the character education program?

Teaching by Example

Now, I'm not sure if it was a sign of character or a sign of a character flaw, but I didn't really do the program. I did my best to introduce the vocabulary words and to use anything in the kit that I didn't find foolish, condescending (to my 8-year-olds), or outright brainwashing.

But there was no way I was going to put a purple puppet on my hand and have him lecture my children on the virtues of being on time. What I thought was that the virtues worth learning could best be taught through example, and I worked very hard to do that—like, for one thing, avoiding false praise.

But character education keeps growing. I read recently that one organization claims to be "leading a national call to character." Another has built an entire program around the notion that "character counts."

Most of the character education-advocate organizations list traits that they identify as the central principles or "pillars" in character development. They usually include words like responsibility, fairness, pride, citizenship. As so often happens in

Indoctrination, Not Education

Let me get straight to the point. What goes by the name of character education nowadays is, for the most part, a collection of exhortations and extrinsic inducements designed to make children work harder and do what they're told. Even when other values are also promoted—caring or fairness, say—the preferred method of instruction is tantamount to indoctrination. The point is to drill students in specific behaviors rather than to engage them in deep, critical reflection about certain ways of being. This is the impression one gets from reading articles and books by contemporary proponents of character education as well as the curriculum materials sold by the leading national programs.

Alfie Kohn, Phi Delta Kappan, *February 1997.*

education, these words are presented as though they represented straightforward, commonly understood concepts—like everybody knows what character is and everybody wants everybody else to have it.

Defining Character Is Not So Simple

But I don't always know what fair is, what responsibility is, what citizenship is, or when pride becomes prideful. And when I do know, I notice there are usually honorable people around me who disagree. Heck, we can't all even agree cross-culturally on what it means to be polite—and I'm not saying we should. But these character education programs never worry about the fine print or about different values and perspectives—unless, of course, those are the words of the week.

I don't want to be unkind. I really don't. But I also want to be honest, and I'm not sure which character trait—kindness or honesty—should win out here.

Many people who create character programs surely do so out of sincere concern and desire to help make a better world. But when their programs present complex and multifaceted virtues as if they were simple and easy, they do a great disservice. And when they pretend that we all agree about what constitutes truth, justice, and the American way, they are being intellectually dishonest.

And too often, it seems, character programs are far less about preparing students to live virtuous lives than about stuff—stuff that can be developed, purchased, and implemented; stuff like videos, booklets, puppets, and large plastic banners proclaiming the word of the week; stuff like workshops, seminars, inservice trainings; stuff like books and lectures and large fees.

One might say that the lessons my siblings and I learned as we drove along the highway listening to my mother's songs of death and sorrow were moral stories not unlike those produced by the character education folks. But I knew my mother.

She was a complex person, and her actions, both good and bad, reasonable and strange, taught me about fairness, responsibility, and other virtues. And that's the way we learn such things—not by building our vocabularies or collecting little slips of paper celebrating our willingness to hold a door open.

| "Teachers should describe competing views to students and explain the arguments for and against these views as made by their chief proponents."

Critiques of Darwinian Evolution Should Be Taught in Science Classes

Stephen C. Meyer and John Angus Campbell

In the following viewpoint, Stephen C. Meyer and John Angus Campbell advocate that science educators teach students that evolutionary theory offers only one perspective on how life originated. While the authors acknowledge that instructors have been forbidden by law to teach creationism, they still can point out that Charles Darwin's evolutionary theory is a subject of controversy and that other views on life's origins exist. Meyer and Campbell contend that by teaching the controversy, students learn how to make up their own minds based on present evidence. Stephen C. Meyer is a senior fellow at the Discovery Institute, a nonprofit organization that examines the crossroads of technology, science, and culture. John Angus Campbell is a com-

Stephen C. Meyer and John Angus Campbell, "Teach the Controversy," *Discovery Institute Center for Science and Culture*, March 11, 2005. Reproduced by permission.

munications professor at the University of Memphis. The pair served as the editors of the book Darwinism, Design and Public Education.

As you read, consider the following questions:

1. As Meyer and Campbell explain, why do many educators feel that they face a no-win situation when teaching about the origins of life?
2. What evidence do Michael Behe and Dean Kenyon offer to question Darwin's theory of evolution?
3. According to the authors, what was the result of the ruling in the 1987 Supreme Court case *Edwards v. Aguillard*?

What should public schools teach about life's origins? Should science educators teach only contemporary Darwinian theory, or not even mention it? Should school boards mandate that students learn about alternative theories? If so, which ones? Or should schools forbid discussion of all theories except neo-Darwinism?

These questions are now arising frequently as districts around the country consider how to respond to the growing controversy over biological origins.

Of course, many educators wish such controversies would simply go away. On the one hand, if science teachers teach only Darwinian evolution, many parents and religious activists will protest. On the other, if teachers present religiously-based creationism, they run afoul Supreme Court rulings. Either way, it seems educators face a no-win situation.

So what should they do? Is there any approach that will satisfy—if not everybody—at least most reasonable people?

Teach the Controversy

Surprisingly, there is a way to teach evolution that will benefit students and satisfy all but the most extreme ideologues.

Rather than ignoring the controversy or teaching religiously-based ideas, teachers should teach about the scientific controversy that now exists over Darwinian evolution.

This is simply good education.

When credible experts disagree about a controversial subject, students should learn about competing perspectives.

In such cases teachers should not teach as true only one view—just the Republican or just the Democratic view of the New Deal in a history class, for example. Instead, teachers should describe competing views to students and explain the arguments for and against these views as made by their chief proponents. We call this "teaching the controversy."

But is there really a scientific, as opposed to just a cultural or religious controversy, over evolution?

In fact there are several significant scientific controversies about key aspects of evolutionary theory.

Evidence Worth Questioning

First, some scientists doubt the idea that all organisms have evolved from a single common ancestor. Why? Fossil studies reveal "a biological big bang" near the beginning of the Cambrian period (530 million years ago) when many major, separate groups of organisms or "phyla" (including most animal body plans) emerged suddenly without clear precursors. Fossil finds repeatedly have confirmed a pattern of explosive appearance and prolonged stability in living forms—not the gradual "branching-tree" pattern implied by Darwin's common ancestry thesis.

Other scientists doubt the creative power of the Darwinian mechanism. While many scientists accept that natural selection can produce small-scale "micro-evolutionary" variations, many biologists now doubt that natural selection and random mutations can generate the large-scale changes necessary to produce fundamentally new structures and forms of life. Over 350 scientists, including researchers from institutions such as

Minnesota Residents Respond to the Question of How Evolution Should Be Taught in Schools

Do you strongly agree, somewhat agree, somewhat disagree, or strongly disagree with the following statement: "When Darwin's theory of evolution is taught in school, students should also learn how scientists continue to critically analyze aspects of evolutionary theory."

Which of the following two statements comes closer to your own opinion?

Statement A: Biology teachers should teach only Darwin's theory of evolution and the scientific evidence that supports it.

Statement B: Biology teachers should teach Darwin's theory of evolution, but also the scientific evidence against it.

Rebecca Wittman, "Minnesota's Science Standards," Zogby International, February 17, 2004.

M.I.T, Yale, Rice, and the Smithsonian, have signed a statement questioning the creative power of the selection/mutation mechanism.

Finally, some scientists doubt the Darwinian idea that living things merely "appear" designed. Instead, they think that living systems display tell-tale signs of actual or "intelligent" design. Prominent scientists, like Lehigh University biochemist Michael Behe and former San Francisco State University biophysicist Dean Kenyon, have cited intriguing evidence in support of this theory such as the presence of digital information, complex circuits and miniature motors in living cells. Recently, mainstream academic publishers, notably Cambridge University Press, have published books and articles that present the scientific case for, and the debate over, intelligent design.

Since intelligent design is a new theory of biological origins, we recommend that students not be required to learn about it. Nevertheless, we think they should learn about the scientific strengths and weaknesses of orthodox Darwinism. Clearly, teachers should also be free to tell their students about alternative new theories like Behe's design theory, provided these theories are based (as Behe's is) upon scientific evidence, not scriptural texts.

A Compelling Approach

There are many reasons to adopt this "teach the controversy" approach.

First, constitutional law permits it. In the controlling *Edwards v. Aguillard* case, the Supreme Court ruled that it is permissible to teach students about both alternative scientific theories of origins and scientific criticism of prevailing theories.

Second, federal education policy calls for it. The authoritative report language accompanying the No Child Left Behind act states that "where topics are taught that may generate controversy (such as biological evolution), the curriculum should help students to understand the full range of views that exist."

Third, polls show that over 70% of the electorate favor teaching both the evidence for and against Darwin's theory of evolution.

Finally, teaching scientific controversies engages student interest and encourages them to do what scientists must do—deliberate about how best to interpret evidence. As Darwin wrote in *On the Origin of Species*, "A fair result can be obtained only by fully stating and balancing the facts and arguments on both sides of each question."

Note: Since the original publication of this article the number of signatories of The Scientific Dissent from Darwinism has risen to over 700. The complete list is available at www.dissentfromdarwin.com.

"Requiring that intelligent design be taught alongside evolution in a science class would require that these teachers directly confront their students' beliefs."

Intelligent Design Should Not Be Taught in Science Classes

Craig E. Nelson

In the following viewpoint, Craig E. Nelson, an emeritus professor of biology at Indiana University in Bloomington, contends that intelligent design—a theory that suggests some biological structures are so complex that they cannot be explained by evolution and therefore must have been designed by some intelligent force—should not be taught in public school science classrooms. After explaining how teaching intelligent design would unwisely bring religious discussion into schools, Nelson claims that the main problem with incorporating the theory would be to force instructors to confront their pupils' religious beliefs. Nelson asserts that in this case, those beliefs might be found wanting because much of what intelligent design finds "irreducible" can be explained by evolution.

Craig E. Nelson, "Design Isn't Science," *The Journal Gazette* (Ft. Wayne, IN), August 28, 2005. Reproduced by permission.

As you read, consider the following questions:

1. What are the four pragmatic problems Nelson believes would make teaching intelligent design too unwise for schools?
2. According to the author, what are some of the intelligent forces that Michael Behe proposes might be behind intelligent design?
3. What two examples of supposedly unexplained biological complexities does Nelson say have been resolved by evolutionary findings?

The controversy over teaching intelligent design, or "ID," in high school biology courses has taken some strange twists recently.

The scientific community has almost universally determined that intelligent design is not science. The U.S. National Academy of Science is the most authoritative scientific voice in this country. This conservative group of major research scientists avoids taking stances on scientifically controversial issues. It has clearly stated that ID is unambiguously a religious position, not a scientific one (and that large-scale evolution is a "fact").

Surprisingly, President [George W.] Bush's own official science adviser stated [in August 2005] that "intelligent design is not a scientific concept." Scientists and science educators almost universally agree that if something is not science, it definitely should not be taught in a high school science class.

Obstacles to Teaching Intelligent Design

A major additional reason explains why intelligent design cannot be required in science classes (with or without the teaching of evolution). Requiring it is an unconstitutional advocacy or "establishment" of a religious position.

A pragmatic third problem results. Any school board or state that requires the teaching of ID can anticipate substantial and expensive legal entanglements. The major organized support for ID has come from the Discovery Institute, a group that includes some scientists as well as lawyers and philosophers. Again surprisingly, the director of the Discovery Institute recently reversed its position and stated that students should not be required to learn about ID.

An additional pragmatic problem from teaching ID is also important. Just as much of the 20th century was the century of chemically based economic progress, it is clear that much of the 21st will be based on applied biology. The evolutionary core of biology has been made even more essential by advances in genomics, proteomics and molecular developmental biology. Each of these fields and more are providing deeper documentation of the evolutionary affinities among all animals. More important, evolution is the core explanation of the patterns and mechanisms they find.

New workers in states that de-emphasize the underlying evolutionary biology will be under-prepared for college science courses and for jobs in biotechnology, biomedicine and related fields. These fields are already driving major economic growth and redevelopment.

In summary, there are four important and common arguments against requiring the teaching of intelligent design. It is not science. Requiring it would be unconstitutional. And, pragmatically, defending any such requirement would require substantial legal costs and also would tend to hold back local or regional economic development.

Teachers' Dilemma

To these I wish to add a fifth.

Each of the many high school biology teachers with whom I have worked has tried very hard to respect the religious faiths of their students. These teachers are quite careful to be non-confrontational with respect to religion. To this end, they have frequently underplayed the strength of the scientific support for evolution. Requiring that intelligent design be taught alongside evolution in a science class would require that these teachers directly confront their students' beliefs. I cannot see how this can possibly be good for either science or belief.

Let me explain.

Michael Behe is the most prominent biologist arguing that some features in cells (cilia, for example) are so complex that they could not have functioned in a less complicated form and, thus, apparently could not have evolved. He terms this "irreducible complexity" and concludes that if it appears that these features could not have evolved, they must have been designed by an intelligence. In a class where ID was being taught, teachers would have to help students examine Behe's claims and purported evidence closely. Indeed, the core process of science is the comparison of the strengths and weaknesses of any unresolved issues that are presented.

The first key problem for teachers and students would be with the nature of any intelligent designer. Behe states, "I strongly emphasize that it (ID) is not an argument for the existence of a benevolent God." He states that "candidates for the role of designer include: the God of Christianity; an angel—fallen or not; Plato's demiurge; some mystical New Age force; space aliens from Alpha Centauri; time travelers; or some utterly unknown intelligent force." He also notes that the designer may or may not be interested in humans, may or may not be competent and may have designed only some details, leaving others to "the vagaries of nature."

How is a science teacher supposed to help students deal with the claim that any unexplained design-like features of the cell might be the result of an incompetent, inconsistent and evil alien or a fallen angel? How can a teacher maintain enough control of such a discussion to assure that the students' various religious views are adequately respected? How can a high school biology class be improved by such a discussion?

AND NOW CLASS, YOUR NEW SCIENCE TEACHER WILL EXPLAIN INTELLIGENT DESIGN.

Mike Peters Editorial Cartoon © 2005 Grimmy Inc. All rights reserved. Used with the permission of Grimmy, Inc. and the Cartoonist Group.

It is inconceivable that any courses that were to incorporate ID could proceed without some students asking about the proposed identity of the inferred designer.

Some readers may feel that I am exaggerating here. I am not. No exaggeration is needed. Note that I have used direct quotes from a recent article by the leading biologist who advocates ID (taken from his chapter in the 2003 book *God and Design*).

When Intelligent Design Fails

The second key problem for teachers and students would arise from a close analysis of the biological examples that were provided as evidence of "irreducible complexity." Behe claimed that the cilia of cells with a nucleus provide an example. This would mean that no part could be removed without destroying the function. But, as was promptly pointed out by reviewers, a number of organisms have cilia that lack some of the usual parts and some are quite incomplete. Behe made a similar claim for the mammalian blood-clotting cascade. But this cascade is incomplete in some mammals.

If ID is to be examined in biology classes, the teacher will have to directly confront its claims that some features of organisms cannot have evolved, as part of the argument for some kind of a designer. Since these claims fail, the teachers will be faced with the largely insoluble problem of examining the claims in such a way that students feel that their faith is not being challenged by the teacher or other students. Nothing will be gained either scientifically or religiously from such a direct confrontation.

It might seem that if some claims of ID can be rejected on scientific grounds, it is really a scientific alternative—even if an inadequate one—to evolution. What makes ID clearly not science is the conclusion it draws. If a complex feature seems to be inexplicable at the moment, ID claims that it probably will never be explained scientifically and so must be attributed to some kind of a designer. There is no logical justification for such a leap—the correct conclusion would be simply that the feature is currently unexplained.

Evidence for Evolution

It would be important to emphasize in any classroom examination of ID that the current set of examples of supposedly unexplained complexity are part of a long series that has failed to hold up. Behe himself earlier asked: If whales evolved from land mammals, where are the missing links? He had the misfortune to publish this query in the same year that the first three such fossil links were made public.

Clear evidence has been found for the evolutionary origins of eyes, of the feathered wings of Archaeopteryx, of insect wings and of many other features that once were claimed to be inexplicable. These evolutionary explanations are made ever stronger by evidence from the emerging fields of molecular genetics and molecular developmental biology.

Any comparison of ID with evolution would require explicit examination of similar past claims. It would also require careful examination of the ways complex structures can arise (often by change in function—extra jaw bones becoming ear bones, etc.). This would in many cases increase considerably the strength of the support presented for evolution in high school biology classes. This is a good outcome, but it can be better achieved by approaches that would much less directly clash with many students' religious beliefs.

Forcing a Clash with Belief

One might think that fairness would require that claims that evolution is adequate must be presented alongside evolution in a biology class. Scientists would generally reply that apparently mistaken ideas advanced by a very small minority of scientists do not merit such treatment. There are far too many such ideas and most previous examples have turned out to be clearly wrong.

I have tried to emphasize that there is another, potentially much more serious, problem. Fairness would require that any side that is presented must also be critiqued. But a direct critique of ID is going to be much more confrontational to students' beliefs than most high school teachers feel is appropriate. I agree with these teachers.

| *"In the classroom or laboratory religious belief should be set aside for the simple reason that the supernatural is an untestable hypothesis."* |

Religion Has No Place in a Liberal Arts Education Except as an Object of Study

Lucas Carpenter

A published poet, Lucas Carpenter is a professor of humanities at Emory University in Oxford, Georgia. In the following viewpoint, he argues that a liberal education should be based on skepticism, scientific investigation, and objective knowledge. Carpenter contends that religion should not be acknowledged as a means of acquiring objective truth and therefore should have no place in liberal institutions except as an object of study. He adds that only those universities and schools that compel their students to think critically and to employ reason should be accredited as affording a liberal education.

As you read, consider the following questions:

1. According to the American Association of Colleges and Universities, what are the four aims of a liberal education?

Lucas Carpenter, "Religion and the Liberal Arts Education," The *Humanist*, March-April 2007, pp. 25–28. Reproduced by permission of the author.

2. What does Carpenter believe is the "backbone of the liberal arts education"?

3. According to Carpenter, in what ways are religious academies misusing the term "liberal" in their mission statements?

Not too long ago one of my better students revealed to me that she was a born-again Christian who believed the Bible literally. Such a disclosure is not uncommon in my teaching experience, and I have heard many students both in and out of the classroom preface their beliefs on a particular issue with "I'm a Christian, so . . ." I've had similar encounters with Jewish students who claim it is "God's will" that Israel exists and Islamic students who adamantly maintain that Israel is an affront to "the will of Allah." But since I also knew that this student was majoring in biology and wanted to be a doctor, I was curious as to how she reconciled her religious beliefs with scientific fact, particularly evolution and the scientific view of creation. "It's easy," she said. "I just give my professors what they want without believing any of it myself." When I tried to point out the schizophrenic nature of her rationale, I could sense her dogmatic defenses clicking into place. "My ministers told me that you professors would try to undermine my religion, but my faith is too strong." She refused further discussion and left my office.

A Liberal Arts Education Should Be Liberating

Something's wrong here. A "liberal" education, by definition, should be a liberating experience, but when a student graduates from a liberal arts college with the same fundamentalist beliefs she had when she entered, her education has failed her. Granted there are now religion affiliated colleges, especially those sponsored by the Southern Baptist Convention, that tout a "Christian liberal arts education," but I maintain that the phrase is oxymoronic, and would be if we substituted the name of any of the world's religions.

The term "liberal arts," encompassing the humanities, the sciences, and the social sciences, has come to indicate study that develops knowledge and intellectual skills as opposed to vocational skills. I therefore use the term "liberal arts education" synonymously with "liberal education." As stated by the American Association of Colleges and Universities:

> The approach to higher learning that best serves individuals, our globally engaged democracy, and an innovating economy is *liberal education*. Liberal education comes in many shapes and forms in the contemporary academy, but in every one of those forms, its aims include:
>
> • developing intellectual and ethical judgment;
>
> • expanding cultural, societal, and scientific horizons;
>
> • cultivating democratic and global knowledge and engagement; and
>
> • preparing for work in a dynamic and rapidly evolving economy.

This definition is obviously generic enough to apply to virtually every liberal arts college in the country, including the very religious ones, and that's part of the problem. With an ever-increasing number of Americans identifying themselves as evangelical Christians (not to mention the roughly 50 percent who don't believe in evolution for religious reasons) and with much more competition for tuition-paying students, most schools don't want to risk alienating any of the students they are so desperately recruiting by saying anything that could possibly be construed as antireligious.

Marketing a Spiritual Education

Indeed, many schools are going out of their way to stress the "spiritual" dimension of the education they offer. For example my own institution, Emory University's Oxford College, recently approved a statement defining the liberal arts intensive education that we hope to make our signature. That statement contains the following: "There must be places in the students' experiences to address effective and spiritual knowledge as well as cognitive knowledge."

Certainly Martha Nussbaum, in *Upheavals of Thought: The Intelligence of Emotions*, and others have made a strong case for affective cognition, but spiritual knowledge must refer to "revealed" knowledge conveyed by supernatural agency. I don't believe the modern university gives credence to such revelations, although we certainly do study them as they have found expression in the sacred texts of the world's religions, as well as in art and literature. The point is that liberal arts colleges and universities are being purposefully fuzzy about the role played by religion in the education they offer in order to avoid offending students, potential students, and their families. After all, the roughly one-third of Americans who claim to be born-again evangelical Christians is a demographic that admissions marketing finds difficult to ignore.

Part of the problem is that the majority of schools in the United States that now advertise themselves as liberal arts schools were founded by Protestant denominations in order to train ministers, lawyers, and teachers. And religion played a central role in the campus life of these schools well into the twentieth century, including mandatory chapel attendance and biblically-based codes of morality and conduct. Atheists and freethinkers weren't welcome as either faculty or students, and faculty were fired for "un-Christian" behavior or beliefs. However, the rise of science in the nineteenth century and the accompanying higher criticism of the Bible, along with an increasing secularization of public life, set in motion a process of institutional redefinition that included the spread of the German research-based university model, the appearance of electives in the core curriculum, and the idea of academic freedom and free inquiry. Religion was increasingly marginalized and relegated to largely symbolic significance.

A Compromise Between Science and Religion

This sea change in higher education was also the result of a tacit agreement between science and mainstream Christianity that gave the former dominion in the natural world as long as it steered clear of the spiritual, a position made possible by the work of John Dewey, William James, and others associated with the quintessentially American philosophy of pragmatism and later articulated by Stephen Jay Gould in *Rocks of Ages: Science and Religion in the Fullness of Life*.

Not everyone on the Christian side went along with the compromise, however. Convinced that biblical inerrancy and fierce evangelism were the only answers to the threat of modern secularism, they formed what we now know as the fundamentalist movement that has led ultimately to the creation of the religious right in U.S. politics. They countered the increasing secularization of American higher education with the establishment first of small denominational "Bible colleges" and then of full-fledged universities like Bob Jones University, Oral Roberts University, Liberty University, and many Southern Baptist institutions that demand orthodox beliefs from both students and faculty.

But the majority of Christian fundamentalists don't attend the most extreme Christian universities (those that refuse to teach evolution) because those schools aren't accredited and hence lack academic respectability. Instead they attend public and private institutions where they ignore teachings that threaten their beliefs. Likewise, the admissions push for ever-greater campus diversity means that many more Islamic, Jewish, and Hindu fundamentalists are taking advantage of higher education in the United States while shielding themselves from the evil influence of the liberal arts philosophy.

These fundamentalists also share one primary premise, and that is that their beliefs should be respected, thus giving them a defense against a full commitment to a true liberal arts education. Often this defense takes the form of demands for alternative writing and reading assignments, especially in the humanities and social sciences. My favorite example occurs in a sociology course taught by a colleague who takes the class to Amazonian Ecuador to study shamanic rituals firsthand. Almost invariably he encounters students who won't participate because they've been taught that shamans are satanic. And because most college administrations are loathe to give any appearance of religious "discrimination," students requesting religious exemptions or alternatives to course requirements are generally accommodated.

Reason and Objective Knowledge Should Dominate Education

But what we're dealing with here goes far beyond religious garb, dietary restrictions, and holiday observance. These kinds of religious beliefs are antithetical to the very foundation and purpose of the liberal arts education.

The liberating effect of a liberal arts education comes not from simply taking courses in a variety of academic disciplines but from observing and understanding how knowledge is arrived at in these disciplines. And in every case the acquisition of knowledge occurs as the result of objective, disinterested study followed by rational argument supported by convincing evidence that produces a consensus among those knowledgeable in the discipline. With that said, all such knowledge is still regarded as provisional, contingent, and subject to revision or rejection depending on new arguments and evidence.

Of course I am aware of the extent to which postmodern theory has attempted to undermine this particular "metanarrative," calling into question such key concepts as objectivity, reason, and the empirical, scientific method. However, such undermining occurs only at the theoretical level. In practice, the epistemology of the liberal arts continues to function as I have described, and science and reason remain the only practical means by which we can manipulate the natural world to our benefit. After all, even though [Austrian American mathematician Kurt] Gödel's theorem appears to indicate that the foundations of mathematics are unprovable, it doesn't mean that we stop using mathematics.

The point is the epistemological methodology central to all academic disciplines has no place for the supernatural. The only role that religion can play in the liberal arts education is as an object of study, as Daniel C. Dennett has pointed out in his provocative study, *Breaking the Spell: Religion as a Natural Phenomenon*. For Dennett, higher education has been far too sensitive to religious believers when religion is the focus of scholarly and scientific study. As he puts it, "It is high time that we subject religion as a global phenomenon to the most intensive multidisciplinary research we can muster, calling on the best minds of the planet." And further: "The spell that I say *must* be broken is the taboo against a forthright, scientific, no-holds-barred investigation of religion as one natural phenomenon among many."

Setting the Supernatural Aside

Let me say at this point that neither Dennett nor I wish to ban religion from liberal education. Students should have the freedom to practice their own faiths and their schools ought to make it possible for them to, with one caveat: because no liberal arts institution can privilege one religion over another, no evangelizing or proselytizing can be permitted.

However, in the classroom or laboratory religious belief should be set aside for the simple reason that the supernatural is an untestable hypothesis. In other words, we need to be clear and forthright in our articulation and description of a standard model for the epistemological methodology employed by scholarship and research in the humanities, sciences, and social sciences, with the concomitant understanding that the standard model itself is always subject to question. We shall employ it as long as it works.

Sheldon Rothblatt, in *The Living Arts Comparative and Historical Reflections on Liberal Education*, cites opponents of the standard model who claim that it institutes "established nonbelief" that fosters "a new kind of secular intolerance." But the standard model of epistemology in the liberal arts and sciences is simply a pragmatic, constantly skeptical scientific realism based on canons of rationality and evidence that has served us well thus far in at least partially lighting our way through the "mystery of being." It is the backbone of the liberal arts education and is the means by which one experiences the liberation for which that education is named. It ought to be emphasized in every course of the liberal arts curriculum.

Likewise, accrediting agencies must pay close attention to any school that uses the word "liberal" in its mission statement and admissions advertising to see if this is in fact the education to be found there. Especially suspect are institutions advertising a Christian liberal arts education. As I have already said, such terminology is oxymoronic no matter what kind of religious qualifier is used, because it imposes limits at the outset on what ought to be free and unfettered inquiry. But as things stand now, the less extreme schools—those that tout a Christian "environment" within which a liberal arts education is supposed to take place and that require a statement of faith from their faculty and students—can receive the same accreditation as schools that don't, thus giving at least the appearance of educational equivalence.

The Proper Place for Religion in Academia

It is dishonest to allow religious institutions to benefit by attempting to ride the coattails of the liberal arts education, as Southern Baptist institutions have become adept at doing. In the corporate-speak of current higher education, consumers

Seeing Is Believing

Leaning into your own understanding—cultivating it, extending it, refining it, adding to it—is what liberal education is all about. The project is to move forward to knowledge you do not yet have rather than to enact a knowledge that is written in the fleshly tables of your heart (II Corinthians, 3:3). The empiricism to which liberal education is devoted—let's assemble the evidence and figure out where it leads us—is well encapsulated in the familiar saying "Seeing is believing." The model of religious knowledge inverts that proverb and declares instead "Believing is seeing." And that is why . . . teaching religion in the strong sense—the sense that would internalize its truths rather than study them—does not belong in the public schools, informed as they are by a theory of knowing that puts at its center a mind that stands apart from the objects of its analytical attention.

Stanley Fish, "Religion Without Truth, Part Two,"
New York Times *blog, April 15, 2007. http://fish.blogs.nytimes.com.*

are entitled to know the differences among the educational products being offered for sale in the marketplace.

Furthermore, one of the most frequently mentioned purposes of the liberal arts education is to prepare students for their role as citizens in a participatory democracy. But as Rothblatt indicates, this involves "more than a skill or proficiency and more than general knowledge" because the objective is "a habit of mind that can only be acquired through long and hard exposure to the correct examples." This "habit of mind," of course, is the ability, to think critically and employ reason and evidence to solve a problem or determine a course of action. It is, in short, what I have referred to as the backbone of the liberal arts education. In fact, it is so important in preparing citizens of a pluralistic society that it ought to have a prominent place in secondary school curricula as well.

Once again, the only role that religion should play in a liberal arts education is as an object of study, and what such study has determined to date is that religion, like art, is a form of symbolic cultural expression with its roots deep in our evolutionary development. Also like art, religion is subject to interpretation and analysis and can be studied through the lenses of history, psychology, sociology, anthropology, philosophy, and, if the hypothesis of a "god gene" bears out, biology as well. However, of most significance to the liberal arts education is the fact that religion and religious belief cannot be used to make or decide truth claims. What this means in the classroom is that faith-based beliefs and scriptural sanctions or prohibitions are not admissible evidence.

Liberal Education Still Works

What I have described as the standard model of epistemology in the liberal arts and sciences is arguably humanity's greatest discovery. I say *discovery* because, even though it was developed and refined over centuries by philosophy which, like art and religion, is a human construct reflecting our compulsion to find meaning in our existence, it appears to be a real link to the world rather than a mythic or symbolic one, meaning that it is a reliable source for actionable knowledge.

Even though postmodern theorists have gone to great lengths to subvert this foundational metanarrative, they have been frustrated by the stubborn fact that, despite many loose ends, it still seems to be working. Being what it is, it constantly calls itself into question, something which would never be countenanced by religion. Only through a truly liberal education can a person achieve the disinterested universalism that has done so much to enrich and expand human existence.

| *"Far more than the mere teaching of facts, true education concerns itself with establishing beliefs and values."*

A Christian Liberal Arts Education Provides a Moral Education

Guenter E. Salter

Guenter E. Salter argues in the following viewpoint that a Christian liberal arts education is designed to teach students to reason, utilize their values, and live more fulfilling lives under God's laws. Salter claims that a proper Christian education gives students the tools to make ethical choices based on history and scripture and thus resist the secular trend of moral relativism. Salter expects that those who embrace this way of learning will become more confident in their beliefs and perhaps have the conviction to bring others to the word of God. Guenter E. Salter is a former dean of the College of Arts and Sciences at Bob Jones University in South Carolina.

As you read, consider the following questions:

1. How does Salter characterize "objectivity" in secular education?

Guenter E. Salter, "The Purpose and Benefit of a Christian Liberal Arts Education," *Balance*, December 2001. Reproduced by permission.

2. According to Salter, how does a Christian liberal arts education help students to understand issues such as capital punishment and global warming?

3. What are the two components of morality, in Salter's view, and how does a Christian liberal arts education balance them?

A student's education is not finished when he graduates from high school. He needs to be challenged and influenced to seek an environment where God can continue to shape and mold him that he might become the person God wants him to be. Upon high school graduation he can exercise one of three options: he can go to a Christian college; he can go to a secular college; or he can go to no college at all. The choice is his, to be sure; and there are various factors influencing his choice. In making the choice, however, a student must not delude himself into thinking that because of his attending a Christian high school, his education is now complete and he is ready to take on the world. He is not! His education has just begun; and by reason of intellectual and emotional temper, disposition, and maturity he is now entering that period of his life in which he will formulate his ideas, values, beliefs, resolves—in short, his philosophy—that will guide the totality of his actions for the rest of his life. This is not a statement of propaganda or a sales pitch for higher education; it is a scientific fact. Numbers of surveys have established that during his college years a student acquires and completes his belief system, and that such system rarely changes after college graduation.

Setting Students on the Right Path

Armed with that knowledge, shouldn't we as Christian educators do our utmost to get our high school graduates into a place where God is most likely to get their attention; where occupational choices are made based on God's will rather than on the expectation of material acquisition; where they are taught that the choice of a life mate is to be determined by eternal consequences rather than temporal benefits? The likelihood that such choices are made correctly in a God-honoring manner is greater in a Christian institution of higher learning than in a secular junior or four-year college as logic and experience teach us.

One might expect, therefore, that a high percentage of Christian high school graduates would flock to Christian colleges for further education and receipt of the benefits just enumerated. But such is not the case. My colleagues and I speak at many graduation ceremonies at Christian high schools every year; and we often find that out of 20 or 30 graduates, one or two plan to go to a Christian university. Where do the others go? More and more of them seem to be going to secular schools. Haven't they been told? Or are they simply self-willed, convinced that they know better? Obviously, choices must not be forced if they are to mean anything at all. But we want to be sure that we do not fail to place before our students the clear alternatives with proper emphasis in the right direction. Toward that end, I would like to discuss in this article the value of Christian liberal arts higher education. May we sound the call, and may our students hear it!

Positioning Liberal Arts Education

All discussions about Christian education ought to start with a clear statement on that nature and purpose of such education, are to promote Christlikeness in saved men, women, and children. Based on the unshakable foundation of the Word of God, the edifice of Christian education requires a liberal arts structure with the traditional humanities representing the building blocks, as these are most indicative of God's attributes and character. The liberal arts are language, communication, aesthetic sensibility, creativity, logic, history, etc. That Christian education should, therefore, come under attack from secular sources is to be expected. They charge that, because of its biblical foundation and orientation, Christian education lacks objectivity. It discourages intellectual inquiry and inhibits academic pursuit, they say, because it lets God's Word, not man's mind, decide what is truth. Thus it appears to them that Christian education operates in a closed system which is neither objective nor respectable. Even some Christians are not uninfluenced by this criticism which is of course without merit. If learning depended on thinking without the benefit of presuppositions (that is assumptions/axioms), then it exists neither in Christian nor in secular education. Everyone starts with an assumed philosophical basis on which to build, because education—that is teaching and learning—does not take place in a philosophical vacuum. Far more than the mere teaching of facts, true education concerns itself with establishing beliefs and values; and that is done with or on a system; it is done consciously or subconsciously. Thus, objectivity in an absolute sense is humanly impossible to attain. Every person is subject to his background, opinions, convictions. The highly praised objectivity of secular education is simply the substitution of an ever-shifting, error-prone human mind for the eternal Word of God.

While the attacks from the left come as no surprise, it is a strange phenomenon indeed that Christian liberal arts education comes under fire also from the right. Though well-intentioned, these charges are equally without merit and totally undeserved. They allege that in the name of academic freedom, Christian liberal arts education compromises faith and morals and—especially on the post-secondary level—tempts students to embrace skepticism, glory in intellectual pride, become morally neutral, and tend toward secularism. Thus intellectual nearsightedness on the part of the critics implies that more education equals less spirituality and that, conversely, the lower a person's educational and intellectual level, the higher are the spiritual heights which he can attain. To paraphrase a popular warning: "Higher education may be hazardous to your spiritual health." Holders of this notion delight in pointing out that most of Jesus' disciples were simple carpenters and fishermen and didn't go to college. But misdirected and erroneous enthusiasm is a poor substitute for reasoned deliberation and validity. If falsehoods on the left are to be rejected, they become no more acceptable when they are offered from the right—sincere though they might be. Let us examine the facts! . . .

No Bible-believing Christian would advocate that God can use only people with college degrees. Of paramount importance is a person's love for God and surrender to Him. Thus a grade school dropout may bring honor to God by his selfless and faithful service, while a brilliant Ph.D. might be an abomination to the Lord because of pride and self-glory. In acknowledging that fact we must not fall victim to the dreaded either/or syndrome. Effective service is not preconditioned upon a person's intellectual or educational insufficiency but on a willing heart and full development of all God-given talents. God deserves—He must have—the best in and of everything. He is not satisfied with less than that. The Bible makes it abundantly clear—notably in Luke 19—what God wants us to do with our talents and to what extent. Acknowledging then the fact that God can and does use people from all walks of life with great variety in educational level and achievement, we also need to be honest and not ignore the scriptural record of dedicated servants who obviously had been the recipients of a thorough liberal arts education as the following examples will demonstrate:

Luke, the evangelist, was not only a competent physician but also an accomplished writer. Reading his gospel we note how his linguistic precision and stylistic elegance impress even in translation. Affirming quite readily that the Holy Spirit is the author of the Scriptures, we nonetheless know that He chose the words and arranged them according to each writer's vocabulary and style. Luke's writing skills bear testimony to his education.

Daniel and some of his peers were "skillful in all wisdom, . . . cunning in knowledge, . . . understanding in science" and proficient in linguistics and foreign languages (Daniel 1:4). They certainly were not born with that knowledge. It had to be acquired through education.

Moses was "learned in all the wisdom of the Egyptians" (Acts 7:22). Knowing that God had elected him to lead His children from bondage, we cannot but conclude that Moses' Egyptian education was a necessary part to equip him more fully for his leadership task.

Paul's erudition is amply documented not only in the conciseness and logic of his arguments and his ability to converse in different languages (see Acts 21:37), but we see it also in his many references to Greek philosophy and literature. We find examples in Acts 17:28; I Cor. 15:33; Titus 1:12; Acts 9:5, and II Cor. 4:17-18. In these verses he refers to the writings of Epimenides of Crete, Aratus, Menander, Aeschylus, and Plato.

Without discounting God's special blessings that rested on these choice servants of His, we must conclude, on the basis of scriptural evidence, that their effectiveness was greatly enhanced—if not dependent upon—their extensive education. Going back to the contention that Christ's disciples were simple carpenters and fishermen, we must reject as absurd the implication that they were not well-educated. They walked for three years with the Master in "whom are hid all the treasures of wisdom and knowledge" (Col. 2:3). Learning from such a teacher who not only witnessed creation but was the cause of it (Col. 1:16) and learning from Him in daily contact provided for the disciples an education unparalleled in comprehensiveness and excellence.

Integrating Faith and Learning

A Christian liberal arts education teaches a person to be at home in the world of the mind and ideas. It helps him respond as an educated person rather than a fool. It helps him understand the problems he encounters in all areas of public and private life: political, social, and economic. It challenges him to the pursuit of knowledge, enabling him to bring discipline and order into his own life and that of a confused society. It refines his ethic and aesthetic sensibilities. Based on the eternal foundation of God's Word, the touchstone of truth, a Christian liberal arts education uniquely integrates faith and learning and, thus, teaches the student not only how to earn a living, that is to provide for his material needs however necessary that may be, but it teaches him more importantly how to live because it has an eternity in view. Having benefited from a Christian liberal arts education, the Christian can function more effectively in his three God-ordained roles as prophet, priest, and king. As prophet he proclaims God's sovereignty, using language that is cogent, lucid, precise, grammatically correct, stylistically pleasing, and linguistically impressive by tone and impact. A person who has not learned how to express himself clearly, logically, sequentially, persuasively, and grammatically correctly will not draw attention to the message but only to his own incompetence. As priest, man maintains proper communion with his creator as he heeds His commands and serves Him. As king he exercises responsible stewardship over the created order. He will do so responsibly, not giving in to propaganda and hysteria, having learned to ignore the siren call of political correctness while basing his decisions on reason and evidence.

Avoiding Relativism and Intellectual Death

Thus far I have discussed the general and comprehensive benefits that a Christian liberal arts education provides. For a more complete appreciation, let us focus now on its value in several specific areas. Our society is feeling-oriented. Rather than listening to reason and critical analysis, it responds readily to appeals directed to emotion. Mental response requires intellectual effort—emotional response is immediate and convenient (a gut reaction), rendered on the subconscious level without engaging man's critical-evaluative faculties. Life and death decisions (abortion, euthanasia, capital punishment) are often made on the basis of prejudice and convenience with but casual regard for our rich moral Judeo-Christian tradition, if not ignoring it altogether. Religious freedoms that were so important to our philosophy-oriented founding fathers that without them nations were not considered to be free are currently attacked and curtailed in the name of misconstrued egalitarianism. Efficient exploration and management of our natural resources (development of new energy sources: oil and atomic, opening of wilderness areas) are hampered by mass hysteria that feeds on rumors and misinformation about the earth running out of resources, living space, and life-supporting climate. For instance, we are told that soon we all will die of skin cancer because we punched a hole in the ozone layer with refrigeration gases and other fluorides. But scientific investigation revealed recently that the thinning and thickening of the ozone layer are cyclical affairs. We hear about global warming and possible melting of the polar icecaps which will result in unimaginable catastrophes. II Peter, 3 tells us that eventually much more than the polar icecaps will melt. The whole earth will burn up with fervent heat—not because of the hair spray we use, but because of God's judgment. Wherever we turn, honest and reasoned arguments are drowned out by a flood of catchy but deceptive slogans. It seems that truth has a chance only if noise and distraction are on her side; otherwise she will not prevail. Frustrated by this state of affairs, the educated Christian seeks for effective measures to halt the accelerating mindless slide of our society into relativism and intellectual death. Christian liberal arts education offers the answers. It teaches a person to examine issues rationally, judge them critically, weigh alternatives, and reach intelligent decisions. Thus a student will learn the meaning of an open mind and how to keep an open mind. An open mind is much like an open mouth. The purpose is to clamp down on something solid. Failing that, an open mind can become like the city sewer, accepting everything and rejecting nothing.

Creating Disciples

Christian liberal arts education also prepares a person for effective and responsible leadership. If impassioned oratory and catchy slogans on behalf of a secular cause reveal faulty logic, incomplete substantiation, or unwarranted conclusions, they are to be rejected as intellectual dishonesty. They must be equally unacceptable under these circumstances if the cause is Christian. It is not the worthiness of the cause that sanctifies the methods, nor does a noble purpose obviate the need for intellectual integrity. The truly educated Christian, as a result of his liberal arts education, will have learned not to substitute opinion for conviction or emotional inclination for demonstrable fact and sound research. Properly informed, he can speak out with clarity and assurance and chart the course that man must follow. He will be able to convince rather than cajole, inspire rather than inflame, edify rather than enervate. All of this will not guarantee him a large crowd that willingly follows his lead. But he knows that effective leadership is not measured by the number of converts he garners but rather by the intellectual, emotional, and spiritual growth of his followers. In his three-year ministry, Christ gathered around Him a small entourage of twelve people. He taught them, discipled them, and poured Himself into them. A few weeks after His ascension, thousands came to know Him through the efforts of those few whom He had prepared.

Teaching Important Lessons from History

A Christian liberal arts education helps a person establish and keep a historical perspective. Although each person is uniquely created by God in His image and individually responsible to Him, he still is a member of his society. The present society,

The Rhetoric of Consumerism

Channeled through various paper and electronic media, the rhetoric of consumerism regularly tempts students at Christian liberal arts colleges to believe that ultimate security in life comes, not from God, but from Mammon, and that ultimate satisfaction comes, not from loving Christ and serving others, but from loving money and serving yourself. Naturally, then, the rhetoric of consumerism leads many students astray from their biblical values when it comes to articulating their educational convictions. They tend to see themselves primarily as shoppers, and they adopt an unspoken pragmatic line of educational thinking that can best be summed up in what I have dubbed *The Student Shopper's Credo*:

If I want to have a good life, then I need to shop for a college in order to acquire a marketable degree, in order to secure a high-paying job, in order to buy a new car and a nice house, in order to impress friends and win an attractive spouse, in order to produce a happy family and to provide for their daily "needs," which, of course, are satiated by more and more of the latest consumer goods and services.

This, of course, is not the rhetoric of the Christian liberal arts college, nor is this vision of the *good life* one Jesus would endorse.

Jeffry Davis and Leland Ryken,
"The Future of Christian Liberal Arts at Wheaton,"
Wheaton College Web site, n.d. www.wheaton.edu.

in turn, is but one link in a chain of generations that reaches from the day of creation to the day of the Lord's return. It is clear, therefore, that man is a historical being. Studying his history, he will learn how God dealt with men and nations throughout the civilizations. It will become evident to him how God poured out His blessings on peoples who obeyed and honored Him. He will also see the record of God's displeasure and wrath as a consequence of disobedience. Thus the study of history, providing far more than mere dates, names, and events, yields—especially under the guidance of Christian teachers—important lessons through proper interpretation of that which has occurred in the past. The "now" generation disdains the study of history as a useless relic of the past. Their cry is for relevance, for addressing "current problems" rather than the unprofitable learning (in their view) about the old Greeks, Romans, Chinese, Charlemagne, or even Napoleon, all of whom have died long ago. The educated Christian, however, recognizes that without a sense of history, man is essentially rootless. Where we are now makes sense only in terms of where we have been and where we want to go. History provides us with such important reference points. We must acquire a critical appreciation of the past before we can understand the present completely; and we must understand the present in order that we can creatively prepare for and participate in the future.

Offering Ethical Guidance

We live in a day of shifting moral values; and the study of ethics does not provide a consistent guide for human action, since ethics is a normative matter. Rather, it is suggested that time, place, and circumstance determine right and wrong in the absence of fixed standards; hence: situation ethics. Men do that which is right in their own eyes. And the Humanist Manifesto II [a document written in 1973 listing goals of humanism in the coming decades] declares that community standards and consensus determine moral values. In the face of such confusion and ethical laxity, Christian liberal arts education teaches the timeless validity of divinely established ethical principles. Christians who teach these truths are derided as anachronistic, wanting to turn back the clock as though progress were measured by the extent to which the relevance of the past is denied. Christian education will teach the student, always on the basis of Scripture, how to make correct moral choices. As he studies his dramas, novels, poetry, and philosophical essays—all of which may be called the laboratories of life—he will come to know that ethical dilemmas are real, and that there are no simplistic answers. Rather than handing him a catalog that delineates the proper action for each situation—a catalog that does not exist because it would be impossible to anticipate all possible situations a man will face in life—proper Christian education will teach the Scripturally correct concept of an ethical hierarchy. Biblical example will provide the proper framework within which man with clear thinking and the guidance of the Holy Spirit will be able to make moral choices that please God. Life does not always present us with clear black-and-white situations. Sometimes duties appear to conflict when at a given time two laws apply but we can obey only one of them, as was the cause with Rahab who was faced with the ethical dilemma of either telling the truth and thereby compromising the safety of the two Israelites or engaging in deception and thus protecting the men of God. Intellectual keenness fostered by a Christian liberal arts education is often required to determine which Scriptural principle applies to a given situation. As we discuss morality we realize that it has two corresponding components: intent and conduct. Excessive concern with conduct tends toward legalism and, possibly, self-righteousness. On the other hand, overemphasis of intent may provide a welcome excuse not to follow biblical command. But the properly educated Christian will be able, by God's grace, not only to make the right decisions, but to explain to his shallow critics the difference between situation ethics and a Scripturally taught ethical hierarchy. Situation ethics has no absolute standards; the situation determines right and wrong, whereas the Christian always approaches each situation with divine standards firmly determined. Yet faced with an ethical dilemma, his obedience to one law does not invalidate the other.

Understanding What Is True Beauty

Another benefit of Christian liberal arts education lies in the area of aesthetics. It sensitizes the student that he may gain a critical appreciation for that which is truly beautiful. Armed with that knowledge he can exercise the proper judgments concerning the things he chooses for his entertainment, enjoyment, and edification. The world teaches that beauty lies in the eye of the beholder and is entirely subjective. However, the Christian has learned that there are absolute criteria for determining what is beautiful, although he may allow some latitude for individual tastes. Therefore, the Christian studies and then applies Scriptural standards as he occupies himself with music, art, and literature. He learns to be alert to objectionable elements in either content or situation of a work of art. This is the development of a discerning spirit. Taking the Bible as his guide and using his critical faculties, he will not reject on superficial grounds that which is acceptable, nor will he allow the intrusion of objectionable elements in the name of so-called academic freedom. Man learns from negative as well as positive examples. The fact that a work of literature, for example, has been produced by a nonbeliever or that it contains some objectionable elements does not automatically render it unfit for providing enjoyment or instruction to the Christian. Of overriding concern must be the explicitness or gratuitousness of such elements and the overall moral tone of the work. The Bible must be our guide here as in all other matters. It contains itself many objectionable elements; yet they are given for our edification. Sin is never treated lightly in the Scripture, nor do its consequences yield anything but Gods wrath.

A Christian liberal arts education attempts to help the saved Christian young person reach his potential; and it contributes to his spiritual, emotional, and intellectual growth that he may become the person God wants him to be: a testimony of God's love and grace; an image of God's attributes and characteristics; a good citizen of his earthly community; an example to believer and unbeliever; the salt of the earth. In summary, he will have learned to be intellectual rather than bookish, informed rather than opinionated, discriminating rather than prejudiced, competent rather than competitive, compassionate rather than condescending, committed rather than captured, and disciplined rather than capricious. Imitating his Lord and Scriptural exemplars, he will have allowed his Christian liberal arts education to help him become "all things to all men, that [he] might by all means save some" (I Cor. 9:22). And that, in the final analysis, is the value of a Christian liberal arts education.

Periodical Bibliography

The following articles have been selected to supplement the diverse views presented in this chapter.

Michael W. Apple — "Evolution versus Creationism in Education," *Educational Policy*, March 2008.

Jacques S. Benninga, et al. — "Character and Academics: What Good Schools Do," *Phi Delta Kappan*, February 2006.

Rob Boston — "Dissecting the Religious Right's Favorite Bible Curriculum," *The Humanist*, November-December 2007.

Lucas Carpenter — "Religion and the Liberal Arts Education," *The Humanist*, March-April 2007.

Edwin C. Darder — "Public Education, Private Faith," *American School Board Journal*, November 2006.

Derek H. Davis — "Character Education in America's Public Schools," *Journal of Church & State*, Winter 2006.

M. Stanton Evans — "The True Wall of Separation," *American Spectator*, April 2007.

Karen Frantz — "School Prayer by Any Other Name?" *The Humanist*, January-February 2008.

Robert E. Gropp — "FYI: Threats Remain for Evolution Education," *Bioscience*, January 2008.

Matthew N. Sanger — "What We Need to Prepare Teachers for the Moral Nature of Their Work," *Journal of Curriculum Studies*, April 2008.

Sherry Schwartz — "Educating the Heart," *Educational Leadership*, April 2007.

Kevin Sullivan — "Character Education Models of Imperfection," *School Arts*, April 2007.

OPPOSING
VIEWPOINTS®
SERIES

CHAPTER 4

How Should
the Education System
Be Improved?

Chapter Preface

One of the debates on improving public education in America concerns the reduction of class sizes so that teachers will be responsible for fewer students. In a 2005 opinion editorial for the *Arizona Republic*, Carol Peck, the CEO of Rodel Charitable Foundation of Arizona, states that the student-to-teacher ratio in kindergarten through third-grade classrooms should be brought down to 15 to 1. She contends that this reduction should first be implemented in schools in disadvantaged districts or where the number of non-English speakers is high. "New research . . . suggests that low-income students who have experienced smaller class sizes in the early grades gain lasting benefits, including a much greater probability of graduating from high school," Peck writes.

President Bill Clinton was unsuccessful in getting congressional measures passed to reduce class size despite the fact that teachers, principals, and students across the nation attested to the claim that a lower student-to-teacher ratio was beneficial to learning. States have taken up the issue to pass laws of their own to limit class size. Michigan is one such state that opted for smaller class sizes in pilot programs in specific cities. Speaking of the success of the pilot program in Flint—a metropolis that witnessed economic collapse when the auto industry began laying off workers—former state Senator Joe Conroy said, "Forty-three percent more fourth graders are passing the state reading test, and 18 percent more are passing the state math test."

Eric A. Hanushek is a leading authority who would dispute Conroy's claims. Chairman of the Executive Committee for the Texas Schools Project at the University of Texas at Dallas, Hanushek has since 1998 contended that research shows no correlation between smaller class sizes and improvements on standardized test scores. In Hanushek's view, "broadly reducing class sizes is extraordinarily expensive and, based on years of research and experience, very ineffective." Others agree that while smaller classes may offer some benefits to students in lower grades (where young children with shorter attention spans may need to connect more with teachers), those benefits are lost on older students.

In 2007 the New York City Board of Education voted to cut class sizes, proving that the issue is still topical. In the following chapter, researchers and commentators offer other current proposals to improve education in America. Some of these suggestions focus on the students, some focus on the teachers, while still others focus on the bureaucracy of school districts. All assume that the present education system needs improving if it is to continue to meet the needs of the nation's young people.

| *"Accountability makes a significant difference in educational excellence."*

"No Child Left Behind" Is Working and Should Be Reauthorized

George W. Bush

In the following viewpoint, President George W. Bush praises the positive educational results achieved by the Harlem Village Academy Charter School. Bush attributes the school's success to its adherence to the testing and accountability prescription of No Child Left Behind Act (NCLB), and he claims that students attending the school receive a better education than they would without the mandates of the act. Bush states that by measuring children's progress, problems can be diagnosed and the education that a child receives can be tailored to fit his or her needs. Using the success of the Harlem Village Academy Charter School, the president makes a case for the reauthorization and expansion of NCLB. George W. Bush, the 43rd president of the United States, first signed the NCLB legislation into law on January 8, 2002.

George W. Bush, "President Bush Encourages the Reauthorization of No Child Left Behind, Speech at the Harlem Village Academy Charter School," in whitehouse.gov, April 24, 2007.

As you read, consider the following questions:

1. What is the importance of measurement in education, according to the president?

2. As Bush relates, what percentage of students at the Harlem Village Academy Charter School met state academic standards in math when the school opened, and what percentage met the standards in 2006?

3. What suggestions does Bush give for improving the No Child Left Behind Act (NCLB)?

I want to talk about schools, and I want to talk about educational excellence for every single child. And I want to emphasize that in my remarks, my hopes of the public school systems in every state and every community excel. That's our goal. The public school systems have provided great opportunities for a lot of Americans. One of the great assets of the United States of America is a public school system that works.

I also believe that parental involvement is an important aspect of having a public school system that works, and I like the fact that charter schools encourage parental involvement. I like to be able to sit with parents and say, I have chose school for my child—chosen the school for my child—I could use a little extra help.

No Child Left Behind in Action

Isn't that an interesting concept? I made the choice to send my child here. That has got a nice ring to it, as far as I'm concerned. I appreciate the fact that the teachers involve the parents in the child's education. There's a lot of information flows that take place between the parent and the child, and the child and the teacher. I appreciate the fact that teachers give parents their cell phone numbers. I think that's an important way to make sure parents are involved in the education of their children.

I appreciate the fact that folks here [at the Harlem Village Academy Charter School] set high standards. I know this isn't all that profound, but when you set low standards you get bad results. I used to call it the soft bigotry of low expectations. You kind of say, well, certain people can't learn, therefore let's make sure the standards are low. This school challenges that soft bigotry and insists upon high standards. And guess what? That's what parents want. Parents want their children challenged. Parents believe that high standards are good for their children.

I appreciate the fact that people go to school here from 7:30 a.m. until 5:45 p.m. That's innovation. That means somebody here is saying, I'm going to adjust the time the children go to school so that we can achieve high standards. I like the idea of schools having flexibility to meet the needs of their parents and their children. Maybe some schools around the country couldn't have that kind of innovation because the rules and the process say, well, you can't adjust that way. What I like are schools that focus on results, and then adjust the process to meet the results.

I appreciate the fact that parents choose this school because it's safe. That's what parents want—they want safety for their children. I met with Vanessa Freemen; her daughter, Krystal, goes to this school. She was struggling at her old school. The teacher said she was acting up in class in the old school. In other words, the parent, Vanessa, recognized there was a problem and—my mother probably got a few of those calls, too—but, anyway, Vanessa transferred Krystal here to the Harlem Village Academy. She's learning algebra. She said her math teacher—her math teacher says her progress has given her goose bumps. . . .

I want you to know that it is a national objective, an important national goal to make sure every child realizes his or her full potential. And that is the whole philosophy behind the No Child Left Behind Act. You know, when we put our mind to it, actually Republicans and Democrats can work to-gether—we did so to get this important piece of legislation passed.

The philosophy behind the bill is this: When the federal government spends money, we should expect results. And by the way, when the state spends money, it ought to expect re-sults, too. Instead of just spending money and hoping for the best, the core philosophy of the No Child Left Behind says, we'll spend money and we expect you to measure and we ex-pect you to post your scores and we expect you to meet stan-dards. Because if you don't, you're failing in your obligation to educate every child.

The Importance of Measurement

Now, if you believe certain children can't learn, then you shouldn't measure. In other words, if you think that, well, it's just a hopeless exercise, let's just move kids through the school system, then that makes sense not to measure—why would you—why waste the time. I believe every child can learn, and therefore I believe every school should measure in return for federal money. And then put the scores up early.

I'll tell you why: I want the parents to be involved with education. And one way you're involved with education is you're able to compare the test scores of your school to your neighborhood school. It's an interesting way to determine whether or not high standards are being met. In some cases a parent will say, this is the greatest school possible, and, yet, when the test scores get posted the reality comes home.

Secondly, I don't see how you can solve problems unless you measure problems. How do you know whether a child needs extra help in reading unless you measure? In other words, the accountability system is step one of a diagnostic process that ends up making sure that each child gets the help that's needed to meet standards, high standards. And so the No Child Left Behind Act, a simple way of describing it says if you set high standards, we'll give you money, but we expect you to meet those standards. And if not, there ought to be different options for the parents.

Positive Results Follow Measurement

I appreciate the results of this school. In other words, it's interesting, isn't it, that the President can come and say you've got good results here—because you measure. Teachers use the assessment to see what concepts students are mastering, and which concepts ought to be continued and which concepts ought to be dropped. The data from this school that you—as a result of measurement helps teachers tailor their lesson plans to the specific needs of the child. Isn't that interesting? The education system tailoring the needs to fit the—tailor the curriculum to fit the needs of the child? That may sound simple, but it's an unusual concept for a lot of schools.

The school has a rapid response accountability system. In other words, you don't measure once and just kind of hope for the best for the remainder of the year—you track student progress closely from week to week. When students struggle, they receive one-on-one tutoring during the school day. If a child struggles, there is extra help on a Saturday, hence, No Child Left Behind. As opposed to the old system, where you just shuffled children through and hope for the best at the end, this school measures on a regular basis to make sure that we're dealing not with guesswork, but with results.

I appreciate the fact that this school opened in the fall of 2003. I want you to hear this statistic: During the first year, less than 20 percent of the 5th graders could meet state standards in math, only 20 percent—wait a minute, that's nothing to applaud for. That's, like, pitiful. Last year [2006], 96 percent of the students from the same class were meeting state standards. One of the students was Kevin Smith. His mother says that when Kevin came to the Harlem Village Academy in

2003, he struggled. And now, she says, "He can do it with his eyes closed." That's a math student right there. Deborah Kenny says, "Our school proves that children can achieve grade level even when they start behind." And that's the spirit.

Expanding No Child Left Behind to High Schools

We can see that No Child Left Behind is working nationwide. There's an achievement gap in America that better be closed if we went America to remain the leader of the world. It is unacceptable to me and it should be unacceptable to people across the country we have an achievement gap in America.

It's amazing what happens, though, when you measure. The percentage of New York City 4th graders meeting state standards in reading has increased by more than 12 percent over five years. The percentage of 4th graders doing math at grade level has increased by 19 points. . . . I know, people say, I don't like to test, you're testing too much. I don't see how you can solve problems unless you diagnose the problems. I don't see how you can meet high standards unless you test.

I appreciate the fact that nationwide, nine-year-olds have made more progress in five years than in the previous 28 years combined on these tests in reading. How about that? In other words, we're beginning to make progress early. The pipeline is beginning to be full of little readers that are competent readers. And the fundamental question is, what do we do in junior high and high school? Do we keep the progress going, or do we fall off when it comes to holding people to account?

I believe strongly that we ought to bring the same standards to high school that we've had in elementary—one through eight, or three through eight. That's what I believe. I believe if you want to make sure a high school diploma means something, you better have high accountability in high schools.

Percentage of Americans Supporting the Reauthorization of No Child Left Behind with No More than Minor Changes

Fifty-seven percent of American adults support the renewal of No Child Left Behing (NCLB) with only minor changes, but only 42 percent of current or former public school employees do. Support for reauthorization is markedly higher when the law is described as federal legislation.

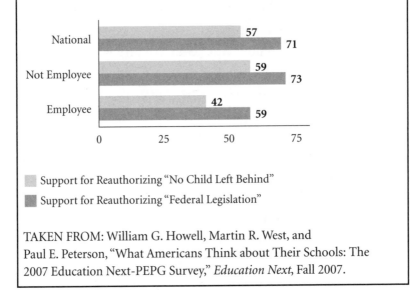

Support for Reauthorizing "No Child Left Behind"
Support for Reauthorizing "Federal Legislation"

TAKEN FROM: William G. Howell, Martin R. West, and Paul E. Peterson, "What Americans Think about Their Schools: The 2007 Education Next-PEPG Survey," *Education Next*, Fall 2007.

We want the high school diploma to say, this person is ready to compete in a world in which the graduates are going to be competing with Chinese or Indian workers. In other words, it matters what happens now in our schools, more so than ever before.

And so part of the initiative to make sure that we continue to set high standards is to bring these standards to high school. I believe strongly that we ought to—the federal government has a role in expanding advanced placement courses all across the United States of America. I'm a big believer in AP. I think AP holds people to account, and challenges people to realize their full potential.

Encouraging Qualified Professionals to Teach

We've got an effort right now to encourage 30,000 math and science professionals to become part-time teachers. Why would you encourage math and science professionals? Because if you've got the capability of competing globally in math and science, you're going to be getting a good job, is why. It's a practical application of U.S. resources to encourage 30,000 math and science professionals to enter classrooms to encourage people to be interested in math and science.

You know, I met a math teacher here. The man went to Harvard—now, we're not going to hold that against him, but nevertheless—he's out there somewhere. He's teaching math. He'd been doing a lot of things, and he's teaching math right here at this important charter school, because he understands the importance of teaching a child math, in terms of that child being able to find good work and be a productive citizen in this challenging 21st century.

Improving No Child Left Behind

Here are some ways we can improve the No Child Left Behind Act. My funding request has money for underperforming schools, when you recognize there's failure and these schools need help. I'm a strong believer in making sure that money follows children. And so when we find a child failing in meeting high standards, there ought to be extra tutorial money for that child. In other words, the measurement system not only helps determine who's falling behind, but it helps determine whether or not that child ought to get extra money now, early, before it's too late. That's been an integral part of No Child Left Behind. It's going to be a significant part of No Child Left Behind as we go forward.

I believe strongly that we've got to make sure that if a school just won't change and continues to fail, that principals ought to be given additional staffing freedom. In other words, there ought to be flexibility—more flexibility as opposed to less flexibility when a school fails.

I think we ought to empower mayors and other elected officials to take a more active hand in improving their schools. If you find failure, it's important to do something differently. And one way to do so is to encourage more power in the hands of our mayors to break through bureaucratic logjams that are preventing people from achieving educational excellence.

And we ought to make it easier for officials to reorganize failing schools into charter schools. We just cannot allow the status quo to exist when we find failure.

Another way we can help is to encourage our nation's best teachers to take jobs in some of the toughest neighborhoods. And so we proposed increasing the investment in the Teacher Incentive Fund to nearly $200 million next year. In other words, there's a way for the federal government to encourage teachers to take on jobs that are important jobs, and making sure that every child gets a good education with a good teacher. The fund rewards teachers who defy low expectations. It provides incentives for people to come into districts all around the United States to challenge the softy bigotry that I was talking about.

Third, parents of students in underperforming schools must have better choices. You find your child stuck in a school that won't teach and won't change, you ought to have a different option. I can't think of a better way to get somebody's attention that we're tired of mediocrity than to give a parent an option. I think there's a better—no better way to send a signal that folks are tired of mediocrity when it comes to our classrooms than to say to a parent, you should have a different opportunity for your child, whether it be a charter school or a better performing public school.

In Washington, D.C., we . . . made an interesting initiative, and that is, . . . we provided scholarship money for poor students to go to any school they wanted. I like that idea. I think it makes a lot of sense. You know, we have Pell grants for poor students to go to college. I think we ought to have federal taxpayer's money to go to poor parents so they can choose a different type of school if they're dissatisfied with the school their child is going to. And so I would strongly urge Congress to reauthorize and refund the D.C. School Choice Program, and take a good look at our program that intends to expand that program. . . .

Bipartisan Cooperation to Improve Education

So now we're in the process of rewriting this [NCLB] bill— reauthorizing it. Here's my attitude about this: one, Congress shouldn't weaken the bill. It's working. The No Child Left Behind Act is working. These test scores are on the rise. Accountability makes a significant difference in educational excellence.

And so therefore, when Republicans and Democrats take a look at this bill, I strongly urge them to not weaken the bill, not to backslide, not to say, accountability isn't that important. It is important. We'll work with the school districts on flexibility when it comes to the accountability system. And I mean that there are certain ways that we can make this—the accountability system—actually work better than it's worked in the past.

But we will not allow this good piece of legislation to be weakened. And if you're a parent, you should insist that the No Child Left Behind Act remain a strong accountability tool so that every child in this country gets a good education. I'll reach out to both Republicans and Democrats again. Last time I signed the bill, I was on the stage with . . . Congressman George Miller from California, Ted Kennedy [senator from Massachusetts], and two Republican colleagues of theirs. And . . . we worked well together.

And so my pledge is that I will continue to reach out and work with the new leadership of the Congress, all aimed at making sure this piece of legislation goes forward, and making sure it's funded, so that we can say, once again, we've got law in place that will enable us to give every child as good an education as possible so that not one child, not one, is left behind in our country.

> *"In one respect, NCLB betrays core Democratic principles, denying the importance of all social policy but school reform."*

"No Child Left Behind" Has Failed and Should Be Abandoned

Richard Rothstein

In the following viewpoint, Richard Rothstein, research associate of the Economic Policy Institute, argues that No Child Left Behind has failed in its mission to provide equal access to quality public education for all students in the United States. Through increased focus on testing and accountability, the legislation has unbalanced curricula and created unrealistic expectations, states Rothstein. Forsaking No Child Left Behind, he offers solutions that he believes could reform the education system and provide all children in the United States the opportunity to receive a good education. Richard Rothstein is author of the books Class and Schools: Using Social, Economic and Educational Reform to Close the Black-White Achievement Gap *and* The Way We Were? Myths and Realities of America's Student Achievement.

As you read, consider the following questions:

1. According to Rothstein, what school subjects have been removed from or limited in the curricula of schools fearing sanctions under No Child Left Behind?

2. What does Rothstein say is the impact of NCLB on teachers' performance and motivation?

3. What reforms does Rothstein suggest would improve the education system?

The next president has a unique opportunity to start from scratch in education policy, without the deadweight of a failed, inherited No Child Left Behind (NCLB) law. The new president and Congress can recapture the "small d" democratic mantle by restoring local control of education, while initiating policies for which the federal government is uniquely suited—providing better achievement data and equalizing the states' fiscal capacity to provide for all children.

This opportunity exists because NCLB is dead. It will not be reauthorized—not [in 2007], not ever. The coalition that promoted the 2001 bipartisan law has hopelessly splintered, although NCLB's advocates in the administration and the Congress continue to imagine (at least publicly) that tinkering can put it back together.

NCLB, requiring annual reading and math tests in grades 3 through 8 (and one such test in high school), represents an unprecedented federal takeover of education. It punishes schools not making "adequate yearly progress" toward having all students proficient at "challenging" standards by 2014, regardless of students' socioeconomic disadvantages or even of their cognitive disabilities.

Lawmakers Have Abandoned the Act

Many Republicans supported NCLB out of loyalty to President Bush and because [Deputy Chief of Staff] Karl Rove assured them that their vow to improve minority achievement would entice African Americans away from the Democrats. But now, with Democratic congressional majorities and a possible presidency, Republicans have rediscovered their belief in local control of education. Few now support reauthorization.

Many Democrats were equally cynical in supporting NCLB. Some believed a law demanding unrealistic achievement targets would justify big boosts in federal spending when targets proved unattainable. Others, arguing that low minority scores result mainly from poor teaching ("low expectations"), expected that federal demands for higher achievement would whip teachers into shape, even if the mandated goals were fanciful.

What few Democrats understood, however, was that test-based accountability might spur teachers but would also corrupt schooling in ways that overshadowed any possible score increases. Excessive testing is now so unpopular that Congress' newly elected Democrats campaigned in 2006 against NCLB and now won't support reauthorization. Senior Democrats are also hearing from parents, teachers, school boards, and state legislators.

Sen. Edward Kennedy of Massachusetts and Rep. George Miller of California, who sponsored the original legislation, promise colleagues that they can fix NCLB. But no fixes are possible. Weakening rigid testing requirements provokes denunciation from President Bush and Secretary of Education Margaret Spellings, who unabashedly calls the law "99.9 percent pure."

Forsaking Long-Term Goals

But NCLB was flawed from the start. The 2001–2002 stampede ignored well-established statistical and management theories predicting perverse consequences for test-based accountability.

One such consequence is goal distortion, the subject of extensive warnings in the economics and management literature about measuring any institution's performance by quantitative indicators that reflect only some institutional goals. Management expert W. Edwards Deming urged businesses to "eliminate management by numbers, numerical goals" because they encourage short- not long-term vision. Peter Drucker gave similar advice. Today, management consultants urge "balanced scorecards" using qualitative judgment, as well as financial indicators, to measure corporate success.

Schools have many goals for students: basic math and reading skills but also critical thinking, citizenship, physical- and emotional-health habits, arts appreciation, self-discipline, responsibility, and conflict resolution. Schools threatened with sanctions for failure in only one goal will inevitably divert attention from others. One NCLB consequence has been less social studies, science, art, music, and physical education—particularly for low-income children, whose math and reading scores are lowest and for whose teachers the consequences of spending time on, say, history, rather than more math drill, are most severe.

Goal distortion has been particularly troubling, as it should be, to conservatives. Two former assistant secretaries of education (under Ronald Reagan and [George H.W.] Bush père), Chester Finn and Diane Ravitch, once prominent NCLB advocates, now write:

> We should have seen this coming ... more emphasis on some things would inevitably mean less attention to others. ... We were wrong.

They conclude:

> [If NCLB continues,] rich kids will study philosophy and art, music and history, while their poor peers fill in bubbles on test sheets. The lucky few will spawn the next generation of tycoons, political leaders, inventors, authors, artists and entrepreneurs. The less lucky masses will see narrower opportunities.

The Problem with Annual Testing

NCLB relies on an annual test, but single tests can be misleading. Every parent knows children have good and bad days. Every teacher knows particular classes can be talented or difficult. Entire classes can be attentive or distracted. So accurate measurement requires multiple retesting. Most schools are too small for statistical confidence that children's good and bad days will average out on one test. Because a school's subgroups (blacks, Hispanics, or low-income children) are smaller than a full-grade cohort, the margin of error for subgroup achievement is even larger. The more integrated a school, with more subgroups, the more inaccurate accountability becomes.

When the Bush administration and Congress were designing NCLB, two economists (Thomas Kane and Douglas Staiger) demonstrated that many schools would be rewarded or punished solely because of these statistical challenges. Their paper derailed NCLB for six months while administration and congressional experts tried to finesse the problems. They couldn't but enacted NCLB anyway, which engendered remarkable anomalies: schools rewarded one year and punished the next despite identical levels of effectiveness; schools rewarded under a state's system and simultaneously punished under the federal one, or vice versa. Some states dodge these absurdities by reporting large error margins with test scores, but this hides poorly performing as well as misidentified schools, and draws the wrath of accountability enthusiasts.

Exaggerated Expectations

Even with inordinate attention to math and reading, it is practically and conceptually ludicrous to expect all students to be proficient at challenging levels. Even if we eliminated all disparities based on socioeconomic status, human variability prevents a single standard from challenging all. The normal I.Q. range, 85 to 115, includes about two-thirds of the population. "Challenging" achievement for those at 115 would be impossibly hard for those at 85, and "challenging" achievement for those at 85 would be too easy for those at 115.

The law strongly implies that "challenging" standards are those of the National Assessment of Educational Progress (NAEP), periodic federal tests of national student samples. But while NAEP tests are excellent, their proficiency cut-points have no credibility. Passing scores are arbitrary, fancifully defined by panels of teachers, politicians, and laypeople. Many children in the highest-scoring countries don't achieve them. Taiwan is tops in math, but 40 to 60 percent of Taiwanese students are below proficient by NAEP standards. Swedish students are the best readers in the world, but two-thirds are not NAEP-proficient.

Expecting all Americans to perform at this level can only set them, their teachers, and schools up for failure. (Actually, this charge is slightly exaggerated: NCLB exempts the most severely disabled, requiring only U.S. children with I.Q.s above 65 to be as proficient as the top half of the Taiwanese.)

In a rare bow to local control, NCLB doesn't enact NAEP's proficiency definitions but permits states to invent their own. Not surprisingly, some define proficiency far below "challenging" expectations, and the Department of Education has little choice but to let this pass; if it enforces high standards, the already unacceptably large number of failing schools would be astronomical. But low state passing points are a sore spot for NCLB advocates, who propose to correct this with high national standards. Their demand makes reauthorization even less probable.

Doing Just Enough to Pass

Any single proficiency standard invites sabotaging the goal of teaching all children, because the only ones who matter are those with scores just below passing. Educators call them "bubble kids," a term from poker and basketball, where bubble players or teams are those just on the cusp of elimination. Explicit school policies now demand that teachers ignore already-proficient children to focus only on bubble kids, because inching the bubbles past the standard is all that matters for "adequate yearly progress."

Less obvious are incentives also to ignore children far below proficiency, whom even constant drilling won't pull across the finish line. Because all must eventually (by 2014) pass, ignoring poorer performers should, in the long run, be counterproductive. But NCLB places no premium on the long run. Educators can't worry about possible distant punishment. And since most consider the 2014 goal absurd, they have good reason to expect it to be abandoned, further reducing incentives to worry about the lowest achievers. What's more, the higher the standard, the more children there are who are too far below proficiency to worry about. So the law guarantees that more disadvantaged children will be left further behind, especially in states with higher standards.

For bubble kids, schools have substituted test prep for good instruction. With test development costly, states use similar tests repeatedly, guiding teachers to stress content they suspect will reappear. Teachers impart test-taking skills (like how to guess multiple-choice answers) that don't deepen understanding of math and reading. In the weeks before testing, schools step up drilling; this does little to help children retain what they learned. Thus, student scores on state tests are not duplicated in NAEP, which is less subject to test-prep corruption. Administered only to representative samples of schools and students, with more emphasis on critical thinking. NAEP scores have not shot up along with state test results. NAEP math scores have increased a little, but at about the same rate as before NCLB's adoption—suggesting that, for all its other problems, NCLB has also been an utter waste of time.

Ignoring Socioeconomic Differences

In one respect, NCLB betrays core Democratic principles, denying the importance of all social policy but school reform. Inadequate schools are only one reason disadvantaged children perform poorly. They come to school under stress from high-crime neighborhoods and economically insecure households. Their low-cost day-care tends to park them before televisions, rather than provide opportunities for developmentally appropriate play. They switch schools more often because of inadequate housing and rents rising faster than parents' wages. They have greater health problems, some (like lead poisoning or iron-deficiency anemia) directly depressing cognitive ability, and some causing more absenteeism or inattentiveness. Their households include fewer college-educated adults to provide rich intellectual environments, and their parents are less likely to expect academic success. Nearly 15 percent of the black-white test-score gap can be traced to differences in housing mobility, and 25 percent to differences in child- and maternal-health.

Yet NCLB insists that school improvement alone can raise all children to high proficiency. The law anticipates that with higher expectations, better teachers, improved curriculum, and more testing, all youths will attain full academic competence, poised for college and professional success. Natural human variability would still distinguish children, but these distinctions would have nothing to do with family disadvantage. Then there really would be no reason for progressive housing or health and economic policies. The nation's social and economic problems would take care of themselves, by the next generation.

Discouraging Teachers

Teachers of children who come to school hungry, scared, abused, or ill, consider this absurd. But NCLB's aura intimidates educators from acknowledging the obvious. Teachers are expected to repeat the mantra "all children can learn," a truth carrying the mendacious implication that the level to which children learn has nothing to do with their starting points.

Teachers are warned that any mention of children's socioeconomic disadvantages only "makes excuses" for teachers' own poor performance.

Of course, there are better and worse schools and better and worse teachers. Of course, some disadvantaged children excel more than others. But NCLB has turned these obvious truths into the fantasy that teachers can wipe out socioeconomic differences among children simply by trying harder.

Denouncing schools as the chief cause of American inequality—in academic achievement, thus in the labor market, and thus in life generally—stimulates cynicism among teachers who are expected to act on a theory they know to be false. Many dedicated and talented teachers are abandoning education; they may have achieved exceptional results with disadvantaged children, but with NCLB's bar set so impossibly high, even these are labeled failures.

The continuation of NCLB's rhetoric will also erode support for public education. Educators publicly vow they can eliminate achievement gaps, but they will inevitably fall short. The reasonable conclusion can only be that public education is hopelessly incompetent.

Inappropriate Suggestions for NCLB's Reform

Few policy-makers have publicly acknowledged NCLB's demise. Instead, they talk of fixing it. Some want to credit schools for student growth from year to year, rather than for reaching arbitrary proficiency levels. Clearly, adequate progress from different starting points leads to different ending points, but growth-model advocates can't bring themselves to drop the universal-proficiency goal. Doing so would imply lower expectations, on average, for disadvantaged children—too much for unsophisticated policy discussion to swallow. Consequently, the "fix" is incoherent.

Growth models have even larger error margins than single-year test results because they rely on two unreliable scores

No Child Left Behind Leaves Behind the Students Who Need the Most Help

If the staff of the Frank M. Tejeda Academy in San Antonio had a motto, it might well be "No Child Left Behind." And because of that, the federal law of the same name is punishing them.

Tejeda only takes students who can't make it in a regular school. It's the district's safety net, offering individual attention, help with day care for young mothers, and an endless supply of second chances: No matter how many times a student fails, if the student really wants to try again, Tejeda will take him or her back.

A school like that can't pass muster with the No Child Behind law (NCLB) as it stands today.

Tejeda [is] . . . unusual. But most public schools have some number of students like theirs, students who face serious obstacles to becoming educated, productive adults.

No Child Left Behind makes these students a dangerous burden threatening to sink the whole school. And the law automatically keeps raising the bar, making success harder and harder to achieve.

Alain Jehlen and Mary Ellen Flannery,
"Is This What Failure Looks Like? How NCLB Gets It All Wrong,"
NEA Today, January 2008.

(last year's and this year's), not one. And accountability for math and reading growth retains the incentives to abandon non-tested subjects and skills. So some NCLB loyalists now propose accountability for "multiple measures," such as graduation rates. But presently quantifiable skills are too few to minimize goal distortion—the federal government is unprepared to monitor, for instance, whether students express good citizenship. Further, any mention of diluting a math and reading focus elicits the wrath of "basics" fundamentalists, such as the president and his secretary of education.

Although NCLB will not be reauthorized, the underlying Elementary and Secondary Education Act (ESEA), with funding for schools serving low-income children, will continue. NCLB will remain on the books, increasingly ignored. Virtually every school with minority, low-income, or immigrant children will be labeled a failure; the federal government will be hard-pressed to punish all. Eventually, under a new administration, ESEA will be renewed, perhaps including vague incantations that states establish their own accountability policies, once Washington abandons the field.

States will do so. Some, not having learned NCLB's lessons, will retain the distortions and corruption that NCLB established. Others, more creative, will use qualitative as well as quantitative standards, relying on school inspections as well as test scores. . . .

Testing Other Aspects of Education

With the federal government proven incapable of micromanaging the nation's 100,000 schools, what education roles remain for a new administration? There are two.

One is to provide information about student performance, not for accountability but to guide state policy. NAEP should be improved. Now given regularly at the state level only in math and reading, such coverage should expand to include history, civics, and the sciences, as well as art, music, and physical education. For example, NAEP could provide state-by-state data on physical education by sampling students' body mass index numbers and upper body strength, characteristics for which standardized tools are available.

When NAEP was first designed in the 1960s, it included important elements that were soon abandoned under cost pressures. While employing paper-and-pencil tests, early NAEP also dispatched field assessors to observe, for example, how young children solved problems in cooperative groups. NAEP assessed representative samples of adolescents, whether in or out of school, as well as of young adults in their mid-20s. Assessors tracked down 17-year-olds and young adults, administering tests to determine if their schooling had lasting impact.

A dramatic expansion of NAEP, covering multiple skills and out-of-school samples, with state-level reporting, would be expensive, multiplying by several times the current NAEP budget of $90 million. But this would only slightly increase the roughly $45 billion in federal funds now supplementing state and local school spending. Provision of state-by-state data on a balanced set outcomes should be a federal responsibility.

Equal Education Funding for All States

The other new federal role should be fiscal equalization. New Jersey now spends about $14,000 per pupil, more than twice what Mississippi spends. Adjusting for the dollar's purchasing power still leaves New Jersey spending 65 percent more than Mississippi.

This cannot be attributed to New Jersey caring more about children than Mississippi. New Jersey's fiscal capacity, its per capita personal income, is over 70 percent great than Mississippi's. And Mississippi's needs are greater: 10 percent of New Jersey's children live in poverty, compared to Mississippi's 29 percent. Again, after adjusting for the value of the dollar, Mississippi still faces greater educational challenges with less ability to meet them.

Washington now exacerbates these inequalities. Federal school aid—ESEA aid to districts serving poor children—is proportional to states' own spending. So New Jersey, which needs less aid, gets more aid per poor pupil than Mississippi, which needs more.

It will be politically tough for a Democratic Congress and administration to fix this, because sensible redistribution, with aid given to states in proportion to need, and in inverse proportion to capacity, will take tax revenues from states like New Jersey (which sends liberal Democrats to Congress), and direct them to states like Mississippi (which sends conservative Republicans). Funding equalization requires political courage not typically found in either Washington party. There's a role here for presidential leadership.

Reforming Education, Restoring Democracy

Narrowing huge fiscal disparities will take time. Whether the next Democratic Congress and administration—if they are Democratic—take the first steps will test whether the party is truly committed to leaving no child behind.

Abandoning federal micromanagement of education has a hidden benefit: helping to reinvigorate American democracy in an age of increasingly anomic and media-driven politics. Local school boards in the nation's nearly 15,000 school districts (but not in the biggest cities) can still provide an opportunity for meaningful citizen participation. Debating and deciding the goals of education for a community's children is a unique American privilege and responsibility. Restoring it is a mission worthy of a new administration.

| "Basing teacher pay on experience and credentials rather than performance means that pay isn't necessarily going to those teachers who deserve it."

Competitive Teacher Compensation Would Improve Education

Frederick M. Hess

Reforming the teacher pay system to reward high-performing teachers would improve the education system, argues Frederick M. Hess in the following viewpoint. He states that it is important to recognize that most teachers are fairly compensated for their work, but he also acknowledges that many of the teachers who outperform their peers are not rewarded. Hess contends that the United States should reform its system of determining teachers' salaries, thereby attracting more outstanding individuals to the profession and, in turn, increasing the quality of education. A resident scholar and director of education policy studies at the American Enterprise Institute, Frederick M. Hess authored the books When Research Matters *and* No Remedy Left Behind.

Frederick M. Hess, "Teacher Quality, Teacher Pay," *Policy Review*, April-May 2004. Reproduced by permission.

As you read, consider the following questions:

1. Based on the statistics given by Hess, how does teacher pay compare with that of other professional careers in the United States?
2. Why does Hess believe that the system determining teachers' salaries today is "manifestly unfair"?
3. According to Hess, teachers of what subjects should receive higher pay?

A rare point of agreement in the debates about how to improve American schooling is that we need better teachers. Simply put, today's teaching force is not equal to the challenge of the new century. The way in which we compensate and manage this force, the legacy of a time when talented women lacked other options and would teach in one school for decades, serves to dissuade talented candidates while rewarding and insulating ineffective teachers. It is time for straight talk on teacher compensation and sensible steps to reform the way teachers are paid and managed.

Even veteran teachers and teacher educators have concluded, as Vivian Troen and Katherine C. Boles write in Who's Teaching Your Children? "The number of good classroom teachers, and therefore the quality of teaching itself, is in perilous decline and will continue to worsen." Academically stronger students tend to shun the teaching profession. Undergraduate education majors typically have lower SAT and ACT scores than other students, and those teachers who have the lowest scores are the most likely to remain in the profession. The lower the quality of the undergraduate institution a person attends, the more likely he or she is to wind up in the teaching profession. From 1982 to 2000, the percentage of teachers who had earned a master's degree in their subject area fell from 17 percent to 5 percent. Professional licensing exams are so simple and the standards for passage so low that even the left-leaning Education Trust concluded they exclude only the "weakest of the weak" from classrooms. While none of these data points alone is damning, together they paint a troubling picture.

Left and right have heralded the need to resolve the teacher quality challenge and meet the federal mandate, legislated in No Child Left Behind, that every child have a "highly qualified" teacher by 2006. Reformers of all stripes recognize that teacher compensation is a crucial element in hiring the teachers we need and steering them into the schools where they are needed most.

Not All Teachers Are Underpaid

It is in deciding how to tackle the challenge that reformers split. Superintendents, education school professors, teachers unions, and professional associations are united in the conviction that the crucial step is the need to pay teachers more. Today, almost everyone "knows," in the words of *Washington Post* national columnist Richard Cohen, that "Teachers make lousy money." There's one problem with this analysis: It just isn't true.

The case that teachers are underpaid is a weak one. Teacher pay is actually quite reasonable when considered in context. The average teacher salary in 2001 was $43,300, compared to the average full-time worker salary of $40,100. While a starting salary of $30,000 may seem shockingly low to some, it's actually higher than what many Ivy League graduates earn when starting in the policy world, advertising, or similar nontechnical jobs. According to the *Chronicle of Higher Education*, for example, those 2002 graduates of journalism and mass-communication programs who were able to land positions earned a median salary of $26,000 if they had a bachelor's degree and $32,000 if they had a master's.

Economist Richard Vedder has observed that the Bureau of Labor Statistics National Compensation Survey shows that teachers earn "more per hour than architects, civil engineers, mechanical engineers, statisticians, biological and life scientists, atmospheric and space scientists, registered nurses, physical therapists, university-level foreign-language teachers, [and] librarians." In fact, the Bureau of Labor Statistics reported that the average pay per hour for all workers in the "professional specialty" category in 2001 was $27.49, while public secondary school teachers earned $30.48 and elementary teachers $30.52—or about 10 percent *more* than the typical professional.

How can this be? Don't we *know* that teachers are woefully underpaid? Let's consider the facts. Most Americans work about 47 weeks a year (with about three weeks of vacation and two weeks of assorted holidays). Teachers, on the other hand, work about 38 weeks a year (teaching for 180 days and working additional professional days). In other words, after accounting for vacation, most Americans work about 25 percent more than the typical teacher. . . .

Good Teachers Are Often Underpaid

The problem is not the total amount paid to teachers but the fact that basing teacher pay on experience and credentials rather than performance means that pay isn't necessarily going to those teachers who deserve it. Highly paid teachers earn their salaries not because they are exceptional educators or have tackled tough assignments but because they have accumulated seniority in wealthy school systems where pay is based on longevity. Providing raises in such a system is enormously expensive because so much of the spending is soaked up by the undeserving.

Some experts urge us to pay teachers more but simultaneously argue that money doesn't really motivate teachers. Scholars like Harvard University professor Susan Moore Johnson point out that private school teachers earn less than public school teachers but are generally happier because staff morale is high at their school, they feel valued, and they enjoy parental support. Of course, this is true. It should not, however, distract us from the need to fix a broken compensation system. While money may not be the only way to attract the teachers we need, it is a useful tool and one we can readily wield.

Rafe Esquith, 49, is a bearded 20-year veteran who teaches fifth grade at Hobart Boulevard Elementary, a school in the Los Angeles Public School system. He teaches his class of 32 from 6:30 AM until 5:00 PM and skips his nine-week vacation in order to meet with students. Esquith is able to offer the extended school day and school year because families choose to enroll in his class. Esquith teaches his charges algebra, gives a daily grammar test, has students reading adult novels by authors like Steinbeck and Dickens, and has the class perform Shakespeare regularly. In 2002, his students read at the eighty-eighth percentile while the school's fifth-graders overall scored at the forty-second percentile. The suggestion that Esquith ought to earn the same salary as any other 20-year veteran is a farce. He works longer, harder, and more effectively than most of his colleagues. Simple fairness demands that he be paid more, far more, than the typical fifth-grade Los Angeles teacher.

Equal pay and equal treatment are fair only if individuals are equal in their effort and their contribution. If they are not working equally hard or confronting similar challenges, then treating them equally is manifestly *unfair*—and that's what we do today. The status quo response is offered by union officials such as Paul J. Phillips, president of the Quincy Education Association in Massachusetts. "Teachers almost never treat salary as a competitive concept," Phillips recently argued in *Education Week*, and they are not bothered "when an ineffectual teacher earns the same salary as . . . high-quality teachers." Our existing compensation system encourages career-squatting by veteran teachers tired of their labors, discourages talented young college graduates from entering the profession, frustrates those educators who pour their weekends and summers into their work, and attracts candidates who are often less motivated than those who got away. . . .

Student Performance Is One of Many Factors

Sensible reform requires, of course, that district and school leaders be held accountable for performance so that they will have self-interested reasons to identify and protect good teachers. Meanwhile, the research suggests that principals who do not have to abide by certification requirements are especially likely to hire and reward teachers who attended high-quality colleges, who possess strong math or science training, or who put in more instructional hours. For all its imperfections, performance-based accountability gives principals a better gauge of employee performance than is available in professions like architecture, law, accounting, or engineering, where evaluations are rendered on an annual basis.

It would be a mistake, however, to rely simply on assessments of student performance to gauge teacher quality. There's more to schooling than standardized test results. Tests are imperfect and incomplete measures of learning, and it's crucial to remember that a teacher can contribute to student learning in a slew of ways that may not show up on a given assessment. A teacher may mentor other teachers or help to improve the effectiveness of colleagues in other ways. She may counsel troubled students, help maintain school discipline, remediate students on material that will not be tested, and so on. We should not reduce the definition of teaching excellence in this way, yet that's a mistake that some reformers risk in their eager rush to embrace performance-based compensation.

It is unfortunately true that apologists have used the imperfections of test-based accountability to excuse ineffectiveness and deny that teachers ought to be held accountable. However, there's nothing to be gained—and much to be

Principles of the Teacher Assessment Program

Perhaps the most promising innovation in the country is the Teacher Advancement Program (TAP) devised by the Milken Family Foundation. . . .

1. **Multiple career paths.** All too often, the only way teachers can get ahead financially is to quit teaching and go into school administration. TAP seeks to change that and keep good teachers teaching by enabling teachers to go up a ladder of teaching opportunities—career, mentor, and master teacher. As they move up the ladder, their responsibilities increase as do their levels of pay.

2. **Ongoing professional development.** Teachers often lack the opportunity to learn from their more experienced colleagues those techniques and strategies that would help them become better teachers. By restructuring the school schedule, TAP gives them time to meet and plan with, be mentored by, and share ideas with veteran teachers. The sessions focus on issues that specific teachers face with individual students, rather than dwelling on the latest fads in teacher education.

3. **Instructionally focused accountability.** TAP has developed a comprehensive system for evaluating teachers and rewarding them for teaching their students well. Teachers are held accountable for meeting the TAP standards for skills and knowledge, and for the value-added growth of their students.

4. **Performance-based compensation.** In addition to compensating teachers according to their roles and responsibilities, classroom performance, and the performance of their students, TAP encourages school districts to pay competitive salaries to those who teach "hard-to-staff" subjects and schools.

Robert Holland, "Merit Pay for Teachers:
Can Common Sense Come to Public Education?"
Lexington Institute White Paper, October 2005.

lost—by going overboard in response. Rather than trying to judge teachers with mechanical precision, we ought to develop sensible instruments for evaluation and permit managers to make reasoned decisions. This is an area where public- and private-sector firms have made enormous progress in the past 15 years and where a wealth of experience is readily available from fields like journalism, consulting, and civil service reform.

Numerous Factors Combined to Determine Teacher Pay

Beyond teacher effectiveness, however it is measured, there are several other considerations that districts should acknowledge and compensate: the relative challenges an educator faces, the desirability of the work environment, and the relative scarcity of the teacher's skills. Educators who take on low-achieving or unpopular schools may find it exceptionally difficult to produce performance gains or to attract students. Compensation and evaluations should reflect such disparities as well as the fact that it's often harder and simply less enjoyable to teach low achievers in a gritty, crowded school than to instruct more advanced students in a well-lit, spacious, comfortable school. For instance, researchers have estimated that Texas school districts could retain teachers with three to five years' teaching experience in low-achieving, high-minority schools at the same rate as in suburban schools if pay were boosted by about 26 percent. Differential pay need not rely on guesswork but can be based on this kind of deliberate analysis.

Similarly, it is time to end the fiction that schools should pay English, social studies, and physical education teachers the same amount that they pay science or math teachers. After all, there are many more competent candidates for English and social studies jobs than for math or science positions. School administrators report that it was "very difficult" to fill elementary teaching positions less than 6 percent of the time but "very difficult" to fill secondary math or physical science positions more than 30 percent of the time. . . .

The Larger Goal of Making Schools Work

In an era marked by the No Child Left Behind "highly qualified teacher" mandate and the more prosaic challenge of finding the teachers we need on a day-to-day basis, simple truths have sometimes been drowned out by calls for more spending or fanciful new academic strategies. The critical first point is that, on average, teachers today are not underpaid. The problem is that good teachers and those tackling the important challenges are underpaid—and we need to find ways to compensate them appropriately. Amidst heated concerns that No Child Left Behind is underfunded and that schools lack the resources they need, the simple truth is that fixing the way we pay and retain teachers is the crucial first step in making schools work.

Moving to a more flexible system of rewarding and managing teachers is part and parcel of the larger national effort to move toward schools guided by accountability and competition. In accountable schools, leaders need the flexibility to monitor and reward personnel in sensible ways and to identify and assist or remove ineffective teachers.

It is in the most troubled systems that commonsense work force reforms will have dramatic effects. In these schools, administrators have tremendous difficulty finding qualified teachers. It is in these districts—with their large numbers of long-term substitutes, burned-out veterans, and unqualified teachers—that new applicants will be welcome, that offering generous compensation for effective teachers or those with critical skills will have the largest impact, and that explicit pressure and individual-level incentives will make a huge difference.

Reforming the teaching force in this way will foster a more flexible, welcoming, rewarding, exciting, and performance-focused profession. A culture of competence will beckon and energize the kinds of adults we want in classrooms: impassioned, hard-working, effective teachers and communicators who know the content they are teaching.

| *"Merit pay arguments . . . seem to insinuate that a teacher's effort is dependent upon his or her level of compensation."*

Teacher Compensation Based on Performance Will Not Improve Education

Part I: Reg Weaver, Part II: Dave Riegel

The authors in the following two-part viewpoint offer reasons why the use of merit pay systems to determine teacher compensation are problematic and are ultimately unhelpful to the broader goal of improving education in the United States. National Education Association president Reg Weaver contends that merit pay will only lead to increased competition between teachers whose students would be better served in an environment that fosters cooperation. Dave Riegel, a sixteen-year veteran of the public education system who has served as both a teacher and an administrator, argues that merit pay plans not only fail in improving education, but also distract from the greater problems that must be addressed in order to make education in the United States better.

As you read, consider the following questions:

1. What corporate example does Weaver use to illustrate the benefits of not using a merit-based pay system?

2. How does the population served by teachers differ from other professionals, such as lawyers and car dealers, who receive merit pay, according to Riegel?

3. Who does Riegel believe should control teacher salary structures and evaluation practices?

An airline wants to compete in the low-cost, low-frills segment of the market, where maximizing productivity and efficiency are critical. The company rejects merit pay. Can it succeed?

If you've flown Southwest Airlines, you already know the answer. Rather than emphasize exclusive rewards, Southwest thrived by sharing ideas, building a strong, unified corporate culture, and—here's a radical notion—encouraging workers to help one another.

Ineffective Legislative Solutions

Many of the assumptions about compensation in the private and public sector are misleading and incorrect. The result is that political leaders adopt misguided pay policies. The Teacher Incentive Fund now being implemented by the Bush administration is one of them.

[In November 2006], the Department of Education disbursed the first $42 million for the program that will tie teacher pay to test scores and classroom evaluations. In Florida and Texas, policymakers hope that an end-of-year cash bonus for teachers will translate into student success.

For all the flaws in this idea, a bigger issue is at stake—the inability of lawmakers to resist political fixes that divert attention from addressing the root causes of the problem.

The strongest incentives for teachers and all working people are competitive salaries and good working conditions.

In a 2006 MetLife survey, one in four teachers cited low salaries and a lack of control over their own work as the primary reasons they will probably leave their jobs within the next five years. Those who were driven to abandon teaching altogether cited frustration with the lack of professional prestige, or with principals who did not ask for their suggestions, did not show appreciation for their work, and did not treat them with respect.

Bonuses cannot substitute for a working environment high on trust and meaningful work. And incentives cannot replace a perverse pay scale in which the average earnings of workers with at least four years of college are now more than 50 percent higher than the average wages of teachers.

Create a Better Working Environment

But there is a better model. Pay teachers for the knowledge and skills they gain. Compensate teachers who agree to mentor newer colleagues. Offer incentives to teach in hard-to-staff schools. Provide group incentives that offer teachers the opportunity to gain greater autonomy and discretion in all school matters.

That's what helped Connecticut turn its struggling schools around a few years back. Today, Connecticut consistently ranks above the national average in math and reading, a turnaround made possible by higher salaries for qualified faculty, increased licensing standards, and mentoring for all new teachers.

A 1998 *Harvard Business Review* article, which provided the Southwest example cited above, substantiates the proposition that enthusiasm for incentive pay far outpaces data supporting its effectiveness: "Despite the evident popularity of this practice, the problems with individual merit pay are numerous and well documented. It has been shown to undermine teamwork, encourage employees to focus on the short term, and lead people to link compensation to political skills and ingratiating personalities rather than to performance."

Don't Tie Teacher Pay to Political Goals

The key question for any teacher compensation system is whether it is designed to improve student learning or to advance short-term political goals. These efforts linking teacher pay to test scores are not part of any integrated strategy to raise student achievement. Instead they represent an oversimplified approach masquerading as school improvement.

Southwest refused to succumb to the myth that the most effective way to motivate people is through individual incentives, and it is the cost and productivity leader in its industry.

Don't let policymakers reduce teaching to the Darwinian philosophy of survival of the fittest. Instead, demand of them the judgment and courage necessary to reform teacher quality at its core.

I was surprised to hear that Barack Obama was sticking his big toe into the merit pay waters. . . . While Obama has not to my knowledge advocated "merit pay" by name or outlined a specific proposal, his apparent openness to the concept has excited advocates of pay for performance who are anxious to see a major figure on the left like Obama defy the prevailing Democratic wisdom and counter the NEA's [National Education Association] opposition to the concept.

Marc Lampkin of the Strong American Schools campaign, nobly promoting the idea that education should be at the head of the presidential discussion, took the NEA to task for suggesting that none of the Democratic candidates in Iowa for ABC's debate supported the concept of pay for performance. However, the candidate Lampkin points to—Obama—was rather circumspect in his support. In saying that pay shouldn't be tied to "standardized tests that don't take into account whether children are prepared before they get to school or not," Obama is trying to have it both ways, giving the appearance of supporting some vague pay for performance standard, but also insisting it not be tied to test scores. There's the rub: a pay system not tied to test scores isn't really a merit pay system at all.

Other kinds of financial incentives, such as paying teachers extra to work in high poverty districts or scarce fields like math or science, can't really be considered "merit pay" systems in the common parlance. Those are incentives to attract people to certain districts or fields. Pay for performance means an adherence to some type of evaluative standard, whether it be test scores or supervisors' evaluations (which are bound to be tied to test scores). And that's the problem.

Teachers Don't Choose Their Students

The use of test scores for evaluation of teachers is fraught with difficulties that should be obvious to any outside observer. First among them, you can't pick your students upon whom your salary might depend. Those in favor of merit pay often use the private sector as a comparison point, saying essentially that most people are paid by how hard they work or how many cases they win or how much they sell. And all that's true. But a salesman isn't forced to spend his time on customers who clearly don't want to buy his products. Lawyers don't typically take cases they can't win. But the logic of paying teachers based on performance is similar to saying to a car salesman, "here are 30 adults chosen at random. Your salary depends on being able to sell all of them cars—a standard car, at that—regardless of their needs, desires, or ability to pay." Or to tell a lawyer, "You must win the next 30 cases that walk through your door, using limited resources, regardless of the merit of their suits, or the expense required to prosecute their cases."

Teachers don't get to choose who walks in their doors, like the hapless lawyer or car salesman in the examples above. It's the luck of the draw. Teachers (good ones) certainly believe all children can learn, and want them to. But success in terms of

Average Public School Teacher Salary by State ($)

Figures reflect the 2003–04 school year

1. Connecticut	57,337	26. Nevada	42,254
2. District of Columbia	57,009	27. Vermont	42,007
3. California	56,444	28. Arizona	41,843
4. New Jersey	55,592	29. South Carolina	41,162
5. New York	55,181	30. Idaho	41,080
6. Michigan	54,412	31. Florida	40,604
7. Illinois	54,230	32. Texas	40,476
8. Massachusetts	53,181	33. Tennessee	40,318
9. Rhode Island	52,261	34. Kentucky	40,240
10. Pennsylvania	51,835	35. Maine	39,864
11. Alaska	51,736	36. Wyoming	39,532
12. Maryland	50,261	37. Iowa	39,432
13. Delaware	49,366	38. Arkansas	39,314
14. Oregon	49,169	39. Utah	38,976
15. Ohio	47,482	40. Kansas	38,623
National Average	**46,752**	41. West Virginia	38,461
16. Georgia	45,988	42. Nebraska	38,352
17. Indiana	45,791	43. Alabama	38,325
18. Hawaii	45,479	44. New Mexico	38,067
19. Washington	45,434	45. Missouri	38,006
20. Minnesota	45,375	46. Louisiana	37,918
21. Virginia	43,655	47. Montana	37,184
22. Colorado	43,319	48. Mississippi	35,684
23. North Carolina	43,211	49. North Dakota	35,441
24. Wisconsin	42,882	50. Oklahoma	35,061
25. New Hampshire	42,689	51. South Dakota	33,236

TAKEN FROM: Dave Winans, *NEA Today*, October 2005.

test scores depends on many factors, mostly too obvious to mention, outside the teachers' control. Not the least among these, and perhaps less obvious to outside observers, is the support of fellow practitioners. In many cases, a child's learning requires the support of others besides just the classroom teacher. It depends on an administrator who can effectively create a climate for learning in the school, it may depend on reading specialists who can help students comprehend their textbooks. It may depend on intervention specialists who help devise strategies for learning-disabled students to make more effective gains. It even depends on successful foundations provided by teachers in previous grade levels. How do merit pay advocates propose to disaggregate the work of a classroom teacher from the support staff around her? For that matter, how would art, music, physical education or special education teachers be judged under a pay for performance system? Would we need to implement standardized tests in those areas?

I could go on and on about practical and logistical difficulties associated with merit pay. But the strongest arguments against it are philosophical. At a time when many progressives are questioning the effectiveness of high stakes testing mandated by NCLB [No Child Left Behind], should we really be talking about entrenching that drill and test regime taking over education today by connecting it to teacher compensation. The real debate today should be about whether the schools created under they tyranny of NCLB are the kinds of schools we want to have. Do we really want high stakes tests driving our definition of education? And driving our definition of quality teaching?

Pay Determined by Professional Development and Evaluation

I am always suspicious of merit pay arguments because they seem to insinuate that a teacher's effort is dependent upon his or her level of compensation. Instead of rewarding teachers for maximizing student achievement—as most would insist they are trying to do anyway—the right approach would be to reward activities that help teachers become better trained and more competent. For example, most local salary structures reward teachers for attaining a higher level of education—teachers who earn a Master's degree earn more than teachers with similar experience who do not. Likewise many states offer annual stipends to teachers who achieve National Board Certification, a rigorous process which requires teachers to demonstrate and reflect upon their classroom practices. These sorts of rewards make sense to teachers: they understand the connection between professional development and effective instruction.

I find that merit pay advocates also hope that a compensation structure will do that job of evaluating teachers that should properly be done by effective building administrators. We shouldn't simply withhold monetary rewards from teachers who are ineffective: we should help them improve or evaluate them out of the profession. The canard that teachers' unions protect bad teachers from dismissal is not true: bad administrators protect bad teachers from dismissal or nonrenewal. But teacher evaluation is more complicated than simply looking at test scores. It requires careful examination of specific teacher behaviors in the classroom, of how a teacher relates to students, and his or her command of the subject matter they are teaching. This cannot be judged simply by looking at test scores, which may be high in some cases in spite of uninspiring instruction: it requires an effective and highly skilled administrator who knows what she is looking for when she observes a teacher interacting with her students, and who is skilled at helping teachers improve. In short, pay for performance provides an easy way out when quality supervision of instruction is what should really he taking place.

Control of Teacher Pay Should Remain Local

Finally, the discussion of merit pay in the context of a presidential campaign continues a disturbing trend of increasing federal involvement in local decision making. Teacher salary structures and evaluation practices are negotiated locally between a board of education and a bargaining unit under the broad general guidelines of state law. If Denver teachers agree to a merit-based system, then good for them. They've decided in agreement with their board on a system that makes sense for them and their community. These kinds of contractual decisions are and should remain local, not the subject of federal intervention. An important reason why the NEA objects to merit pay proposals is precisely this—that it takes away control from a local bargaining unit to decide their own fate. If Barack Obama truly believes that education proposals need the support of teachers, then those proposals should continue to be locally decided, not a subject of debate in a national election, unless it is clear that the debate is purely philosophical, and not bearing on any public policy he would enact as president. The federal government certainly has an important role in education. It establishes policies and guidelines that protect the education of handicapped children, for example, and provides funding to support that education. The federal government supports research in education and provides grants to support high-poverty schools. But dictating the terms of local teaching contracts should not be a function of federal policy.

The debate about merit pay isn't the debate we need to be having right now. With the demands for charters and vouchers from the right, and the ongoing problems facing education in high-poverty districts, the very existence of public education is being threatened. We need to be talking about why public education still matters, and what it should look like in the 21st century. Gimmicks like pay for performance are only getting us off track.

| *"Charters are transforming urban education and tackling head-on the stubborn achievement gap."*

Charter Schools Improve Education

Margaret Spellings

Margaret Spellings is the U.S. Secretary of Education. In the following viewpoint, she presents the benefits of charter schools before the National Charter Schools Conference. Charter schools are nontraditional public schools. Although they are funded with public money, they have been freed from district regulations and some state laws in exchange for greater accountability to achieve performance results set forth in the charter. Spellings argues that the achievements of minority and low-income students in charter schools speak to the possibility of their broader use in the education system. Additionally, Spellings contends that only through continued legislative support, provided by the pending reauthorization of No Child Left Behind, will the full potential of charter schools be realized.

Margaret Spellings, "Remarks at the 2007 National Charter Schools Conference," in www.ed.gov, April 27, 2007.

As you read, consider the following questions:

1. According to Spellings, what percentage of students in the cities of Washington, D.C., and New Orleans attend charter schools?

2. Spellings states that charters are becoming more popular among parents, students, and politicians of which political party?

3. What are some ways that Spellings says the reauthorization proposals of No Child Left Behind will support the progress of charters?

[2007] marks the 15th anniversary of the opening of the first charter school, the City Academy High School in St. Paul, Minnesota. Think about how much has been achieved in just 15 years.

Since teachers founded and students helped design the City Academy in 1992, the charter movement has revolutionized the education world, proving to detractors time and again that charters are here to stay.

We are seeing charter schools flourishing all over the country, serving over a million American students.

In my neck of the woods, Washington, DC, more than one out of four public school students attend a charter school—that's about 18,000 students—and this number grows every year!

School choice in DC is also being bolstered by the first-ever federally funded opportunity scholarship programs—thanks to this program, more than 1,800 DC students from economically disadvantaged families are realizing their potential at 58 private schools.

Cities like Washington, DC, and New Orleans—where more than 60% of public school students attend charters—are proving that charter schools can be very effective at scale. They're not just solutions for small portions of a community's students anymore.

Charters for America's Minority Students

America continues to face a tragic inequity of opportunity in education that charters can help address. Fifteen percent of our high schools produce more than half of our nation's dropouts, and many of these are city schools serving mostly minorities.

Of those who graduate, many are not ready for college. Only 9 percent of low-income students earn college degrees by age 24, and this must change.

Charters are transforming urban education and tackling head-on the stubborn achievement gap. For example, the customization of learning that charter schools allow is translating into improved academic growth among Hispanics, a key demographic group in this country.

The National Alliance reported on this phenomenon in detail last fall, describing how certain charters are customizing learning for Hispanics—from staff, to curricula, to classroom values—and producing great results.

This is especially hopeful news given the fact that Hispanics are a growing proportion of our population. As it stands, about one in every two Hispanic students drops out of high school, and we need to enlist every tool in our arsenal to reverse this trend.

Bipartisan Support for Charters

But it's not just certain types of students who are thriving in charter schools—these schools are booming in cities and rural areas and are serving every race and background.

As charters grow more popular among parents and students, charters are also gaining growing bipartisan support. Look at Indianapolis. Mayor Bart Peterson, a Democrat and the only mayor in the nation with the authority to authorize charter schools, has taken a leadership role in creating 16 charter schools serving about 4,000 students. He's building on the work of Republicans like Steve Goldsmith before him. Or take New York. Governor Eliot Spitzer, also a Democrat, recently succeeded in doubling the New York state cap on charters to 200 schools, while Mayor Bloomberg, a Republican, is giving principals greater autonomy to manage their schools, in return for increased accountability.

More Students Need Access to Charter Schools

Amid all the success and remarkable progress of charter schools, it's easy to be lulled into thinking that the heavy lifting is done, that continued progress is inevitable. But that's far from the case.

Charter schools have yet to realize their full potential, and the public is only going to expect more from charters as these schools gain the advantages of experience and great results. There is still more to do.

One challenge is access, an issue I know you're all painfully aware of. Over a million students attend charters, but many more students remain locked out of the opportunities to attend one of these innovative schools.

All three of the successful charters I mentioned visiting have waiting lists or lottery systems to get in.

You shouldn't have to win the lottery to send your child to a great, high-performing school.

Ten states still have no charter schools at all. It's ironic that the Bill and Melinda Gates Foundation does so much good work to promote the promise of charter schools. But as Mr. Gates recently pointed out in a speech he gave, his own state of Washington keeps them from being able to do this work in his own backyard.

Twenty-five states have restrictions that limit charter school growth in some way. Charter schools have created an educational product that parents and students want, but many children remain cut off from these opportunities.

This must change—we shouldn't be rationing opportunity.

Charter Schools Provide Excellent Education Opportunities for Hispanic Students

Located about a dozen miles from the Mexican border in Texas, IDEA Academy was established in 2000 to provide a high-quality public education to the children of the Rio Grande Valley. Like many public schools in this community, IDEA primarily serves students that are Hispanic (94% at IDEA) and economically disadvantaged (80%).

But there's something fundamentally different about IDEA: Extremely high expectations and results for its students. "There's nothing they can't do," according to IDEA founder and head Tom Torkelson. The school's results prove the point. From 2003 to 2005, the percentage of IDEA's students who achieved proficiency on the state reading test was 88%, 91%, and 90%, respectively. On the math test, the results were similarly impressive. IDEA bested the state proficiency average on 10 of 12 reading and math tests.

IDEA is part of an emerging phenomenon within public education: high-quality public charter schools that are achieving spectacular results with Hispanic students. These schools are capitalizing on their autonomy to customize their budgets, staff, schedules, curriculum materials, and instructional methods based upon the unique needs of their students. They reach out to parents and community members in significant ways, addressing several values particularly important to the Hispanic community, such as dignity, respect, and love.

Todd Ziebarth,
National Alliance for Public Charter Schools,
November 2006.

Charter Schools Continually Improve

In addition to improving access, an increasingly urgent challenge for charter schools will be to provide quality without letting up on growth and innovation.

Charter schools are accountable by their very nature, since they must close if they are not satisfying their customers, but charters must continue to push themselves to deliver the highest caliber of education.

Fortunately, charter schools are up to the challenge! You all are poised to take advantage of data and knowledge about best practices that the first charters could have only dreamed about.

Many charters are already pioneering innovative uses of data. Take a look at the Brighter Choice Schools in Albany. They are using real-time data-driven decision making—evaluating students on an ongoing basis in every major subject and adjusting instructional strategies. . . .

And we at the Department of Education will continue to support you and do our part to help charter schools live up to their potential and replicate proven models.

NCLB and Charter Schools

Over the past five years, we have seen the No Child Left Behind (NCLB) profoundly change education for the better. Scores are up, and achievement gaps are starting to shrink, especially with our younger students.

NCLB is up for renewal this year, and our reauthorization proposals build on this progress and reflect what five years of implementation have taught us. Among these changes are provisions that both help charters and reflect what we've learned from them.

These include supporting local decisions to reopen underperforming schools in need of restructuring as charters, regardless of charter cap restrictions; allowing qualified charter school authorizers to apply for Charter School Program funds that they can grant to new schools; and boosting the replication of high quality charters.

On that last point, I'm pleased to let you know that my Department is drafting revised guidance to give states further encouragement and flexibility to help more high quality charters flourish. . . .

In addition to measures aimed specifically at charter schools, we are proposing a number of changes consistent with the spirit of charters.

On the flexibility front, we plan to allow the use of growth models to track individual student progress from year-to-year and monitor achievement gaps.

And to help deal with the pressing problem of restructuring schools, we have developed a menu of options for local school officials to choose from, including real governance changes and—as I mentioned—the option of reinventing these schools as charters, regardless of arbitrary caps.

American Education Needs Innovation

For all the innovations in education in America in the past fifteen years, so much about our approach to education still looks more like 19th-century agrarian America than the nation that gave birth to Microsoft and Google.

The demands of the 21st century are not going to wait—we need every student to achieve their potential today.

Charter schools are proving that new approaches to education can work—that breaking tradition and taking risks can yield tremendous results for students.

And I encourage you and I thank you for this vital work. Your efforts are helping more and more students reach their full potential.

America has always been the world's innovation leader—pioneering the frontiers of space, medicine, and global communications. And if we give our students the skills they need to succeed, we can be sure that they will continue to lead the charge on the frontiers of the future.

> *"San Francisco has adopted a school district financing system that mimics a school market and has led to a revitalization of the city's public schools."*

Decentralized School Districts Improve Public Education

Lisa Snell

In the viewpoint that follows, Lisa Snell contends that the decentralization of public schools in San Francisco and other cities has sparked true educational reform and improvement. She states that decentralized school districts allow parents to enroll their children in school districts based not on their address but instead on the unique qualities and programs offered by a particular school. Additionally, she describes how public funding is allotted to the schools on a per student basis, ensuring that schools remain competitive. The author maintains that this type of school districting is the most effective way to ensure quality education for all U.S. students while keeping education public. Snell serves as the director of education policy at the Reason Foundation, a libertarian public policy research institution, and has authored numerous articles on education issues.

As you read, consider the following questions:

1. According to Snell, how are schools funded under the weighted student formula that was first introduced by Arlene Ackerman in Edmonton, Alberta?

2. What evidence does the author give to show the improvement of San Francisco schools that have been decentralized?

3. As Snell relates, UCLA researcher William Ouchi states that true local control can only occur when?

Imagine a city with authentic public school choice—a place where the location of your home doesn't determine your child's school. The first place that comes to mind probably is not San Francisco. But that city boasts one of the most robust school choice systems in the nation.

Caroline Grannan, a public school advocate and super-involved parent, lobbied hard to wear down the San Francisco school district back in 1996 and get her son William, then an incoming kindergartner, out of his assigned neighborhood school, Miraloma Elementary, and into a "more desirable" alternative school called Lakeshore. In 1996 Miraloma had low test scores and a low-income student body bused in from other neighborhoods; its middle-class neighbors shunned it. Lakeshore had a better reputation and higher student performance.

From Five Choice Schools to a District Full

Once, Grannan remembers, it was conventional wisdom in San Francisco that there were only five decent public schools in the city; if you couldn't get your child into one of them, it was time to move to the suburbs or to find a private academy. But a lot has changed since 1996. Today Grannan could send her child to any school within the city. What's more, she would happily send her kids to Miraloma, one of many elementary schools in San Francisco that now attract eager middle-class clients. Miraloma has a new principal with a parent-friendly attitude, has begun to raise its test scores, and is more diversified. Families now feel secure taking advantage of Miraloma's long-standing positive attributes, including its small size and its sheltered and attractive setting.

Grannan's more recent experience with her children's middle school also reflects how San Francisco schools have changed. Her son William just graduated from Aptos Middle School, and her daughter Anna started sixth grade there this year. This school is now in high demand, but in 1996 parents considered it dirty, dangerous, and academically weak. Today it offers enriched language, arts, and music programs, and its test scores continue to improve.

Grannan is more than just a concerned parent. She is a founding member of the San Francisco chapter of Parents for Public Schools, a PTA board member, and a prolific writer whose articles about local schools appear in the San Francisco Examiner and other publications. She has argued passionately against both vouchers and charter schools, and would wince to be portrayed as a partisan of school choice. Yet she has become an avid supporter of the San Francisco system and the benefits it brings to San Francisco families.

San Francisco is one of a handful of public school districts across the nation that mimic an education market. In these districts, the money follows the children, parents have the right to choose their children's public schools and leave underperforming schools, and school principals and communities have the right to spend their school budgets in ways that make their schools more desirable to parents. As a result, the number of schools parents view as "acceptable" has increased greatly in the last several years. In Grannan's words, "Parents who are willing to go beyond the highest-status schools can now easily find many more acceptable options, and can avoid the fight for a few coveted seats in the most prestigious schools."

Funds Determined by Enrollment

Give credit to Arlene Ackerman, San Francisco's superintendent of schools since 2000. Ackerman introduced the weighted
student formula, pioneered in Edmonton, Alberta, in 1976,
which allows money to follow students to the schools they
choose while guaranteeing that schools with harder-to-educate
kids (low-income students, language learners, low achievers)
get more funds. Ackerman also introduced site-based budgeting, so that school communities, not the central office, determine how to spend their money. Finally, she worked to create
a true open-enrollment student assignment system that gives
parents the right to choose their children's schools.

In San Francisco the weighted student formula gives each
school a foundation allocation that covers the cost of a
principal's salary and a clerk's salary. The rest of each school's
budget is allocated on a per student basis. There is a base
amount for the "average student," with additional money assigned based on individual student characteristics: grade level,
English language skills, socioeconomic status, and special education needs. These weights are assigned as a percentage of
the base funding. For example, a kindergartner would receive
funding 1.33 times the base allocation, while a low-income
kindergartner would receive an additional 0.09 percent of the
base allocation. In 2005–06 San Francisco's base allocation was
$2,561. Therefore, the kindergartner would be worth $3,406,
and the low-income kindergartner would generate an additional $230 for his school.

The Incentive to Offer Unique Programs

The more students a school attracts, the bigger the school's
budget. So public schools in San Francisco now have an incentive to differentiate themselves from one another. Every
parent can look through an online catalog of niche schools
that include Chinese, Spanish, and Tagalog language immersion schools, college preparatory schools, performing arts
schools that collaborate with an urban ballet and symphony,

schools specializing in math and technology, traditional neighborhood schools, and a year-round school based on multiple-intelligence theory. Each San Francisco public school is unique. The number of students, the school hours, the teaching style, and the program choices vary from site to site.

The pressure to attract children has produced not just a greater variety of unique schools but new school capacity based on the specific demands of parents. For example, as demand has exceeded the number of available seats the district has added more Chinese and Spanish dual-language immersion programs. The weighted formula ensures that schools have an incentive to recruit and serve students with learning disabilities, limited English proficiency, and other difficulties.

All this diversity is useless if parents don't know about it, so schools have an incentive to market their programs as well. Much of the marketing is done through a local chapter of Parents for Public Schools. The district and the chapters host school enrollment fairs, and the schools offer parent tours throughout the school year. Parents can select up to seven schools on their enrollment application. In the 2005–06 school year 84 percent of parents received one of the schools they listed, with 63 percent receiving their first-choice school. More than 40 percent of the city's children now attend schools outside their neighborhoods.

Decentralized school management is a growing trend in the United States. To date the weighted student formula has been implemented in Cincinnati, Houston, St. Paul, San Francisco, Seattle, and Oakland. This year a weaker version that does not include school choice is being implemented statewide in Hawaii, and pilot programs are underway in Boston, Chicago, and New York City.

Refining the Decentralized Model

By contrast, most districts in the United States use a staffing ratio model, in which the central office directs school sites to spend their resources in a particular way, through allocations of staff and a small supplies budget. For example, a school might be sent one teacher for every 28 students. This system gives individual institutions little control over their financial resources and personnel choices. Under the weighted student formula, each school site receives a budget denominated in dollars instead of positions and decides what staff and non-staff items to purchase with that money. Oakland, which completed its first year of the weighted student formula in 2004–05, is taking the decentralized concept further than any district in the United States. Edmonton, San Francisco, and the others all charge each school not for the actual salary of each teacher but for "average teacher salaries" in the district. This means that, for the sake of school budgets, differences in teacher salaries are ignored; on paper, a first-year teacher costs the same as a 30-year veteran. This practice hides funding inequities within districts where more desirable schools are stacked with senior teachers and other institutions are staffed with less experienced instructors. In practice, schools with lower-paid teachers end up subsidizing schools with higher-paid teachers. In Oakland, by contrast, schools are charged the actual cost of their employees, so a school with more novice educators has more money left over to pay for training or supplies or even to hire another teacher and reduce class size—all of which could make a school more attractive to potential students.

Another way some districts go further than San Francisco is in the extent to which parents are allowed to choose their children's schools. Edmonton's system is particularly robust, allowing students to apply directly to any school in the system. Similarly, Cincinnati's high school open enrollment system allows students to apply directly to 26 different high school programs on a first come, first served basis. Such systems stand in stark contrast to the form of choice embedded in the federal No Child Left Behind Act. Under federal law students in failing schools are guaranteed the right to transfer to a school that isn't failing. But districts have not made a good-faith effort to implement public school choice. In New York City this year, for example, 11,000 kids applied to leave failing city schools, but only 2,250 city kids received one of their choices. Since the No Child Left Behind Act was passed, fewer than 2 percent of parents nationwide have used the law's provisions to transfer their children to other public schools.

School closure is another prominent feature of the weighted student formula model. In Edmonton, if a school declines to the point that it can't cover its expenses with the per student money, the principal is removed and the remaining teachers and facilities are assigned to a strong principal—or the school is closed altogether, and the staff is moved to other, more successful schools. The San Francisco school district closed five schools in 2005 because of underenrollment and is considering closing or consolidating 19 other schools.

Improvement Is Evident

San Francisco's system produced significant academic success for the children in the district. Miraloma Elementary, the school Caroline Grannan would not consider for her children in 1996, has seen test scores for second-graders in English language improve from 10 percent proficient in 2003 to 47 percent proficient in 2005. "Now's the time to get in on the ground floor of one of the most up-and-coming schools in San Francisco," one Miraloma parent recently wrote in an anonymous review for greatschools.net. "Student achievement is rising, parent involvement is soaring and the entire community is working very well together to improve the quality of every aspect of the school. . . . Parents are moving their kids from private schools to Miraloma because they like what they see. Yes, there is still work to be done but I am very confident that Miraloma will be the next Rooftop or Alvarado." (Rooftop and Alvarado are two previously average schools that are now considered top-notch by parents due to high student achieve-ment.) Greatschools.net had 19 similarly positive reviews for Miraloma.

Similarly, at Aptos Middle School, where Grannan's daughter started this year, the share of students scoring proficient in English language increased from 29 percent in 2002 to nearly 50 percent in 2004–05. Aptos is also the most ethnically diverse school in the district: Its demographic composition in 2004–05 was 26 percent Hispanic, 32 percent Asian, 19 percent black, 13 percent white, 6 percent Filipino, 3 percent multiracial, and 1 percent Native American. Close to 50 percent of the students participate in the federal free lunch program, which is the standard proxy for poverty in public schools—schools with large free lunch populations generally have a more difficult time with academic achievement. California's academic performance index (API) ranks a student body's performance on several standardized tests. Aptos' score has just risen from 6 out of 10 to 7 out of 10 (10 is best); it ranks 8 out of 10 when compared to schools with similar demographics.

Such gains have been made throughout the school district. Every grade level in San Francisco has seen increases in student achievement in math and language arts, and the district is scoring above state averages. (Fifty percent of San Francisco seventh-graders were proficient in language arts in 2005, compared to 37 percent proficiency statewide.) Even high schools, the most intractable of all schools, appear to be improving. Mission made *Newsweek*'s 2005 list of the nation's top 1,000 high schools. Galileo has shown a big jump in test scores—its statewide API ranking jumped from a 3 to a 6 in just one year, while its ranking compared to similar schools climbed from a 2 to an 8. Balboa is on the radar for families who never would have considered it a few years ago.

These gains have been made even as students who used to be excluded from standardized tests are increasingly being

The Interest in Decentralized Decisionmaking for Schools

Interest in decentralizing education is a worldwide phenomenon, and the theoretical reasons for pursuing this reform remain as powerful today as when they were first developed. Public education systems are bureaucracies, and bureaucracies, with their codified rules and standardized procedures specifying how work is to be done, are increasingly seen as problematic in "environments [like schools] in which circumstances change often, clients' needs are difficult to predict precisely, and/or the tasks being performed are not standardized." Bureaucracies discourage creativity and innovation and encourage a focus on compliance with rules.

Decentralizing decisionmaking as close as possible to the organizational level where key services are performed has been viewed, inside and outside of education, as a way to increase efficiency and spur adoption of more-effective means of reaching performance goals. Much of the interest in decentralization among educators was inspired by the experience of businesses that, when faced with unprecedented levels of global competition in the late 20th century, dramatically reformed their traditionally top-down structures in imitation of so-called "quality" approaches to management. Organizational and management scholars have cited both theoretical and empirical evidence to support claims that decentralized organizations perform at higher levels than centralized ones.

Janet S. Hansen and Marguerite Roza,
"Decentralized Decisionmaking for Schools:
New Promise for an Old Idea?"
RAND Occasional Paper Series, *2005.*

tested. In the last year of Superintendent Bill Rojas' administration, 1998–99, only 77 percent of the district's students in the tested grades were included, with kids who were deemed likely to bring scores down left out whenever possible. In 2003–04, 98 percent of students in the tested grades were included.

A Nationwide Trend

San Francisco is not alone. William Ouchi of UCLA's Anderson School of Management has done extensive research on the effects of school district decentralization throughout the United States. Ouchi and his team of 12 researchers studied three very centralized public school districts: New York City, Los Angeles, and Chicago; three very decentralized public school districts that used the weighted student formula: Seattle, Houston, and Edmonton; and three very decentralized Catholic school systems: Chicago, New York City, and Los Angeles. In his 2003 book *Making Schools Work*, Ouchi found that the decentralized public school districts and private Catholic schools had significantly less fraud, less centralized bureaucracy and staff, more money at the classroom level, and higher student achievement.

He also found that most districts merely give lip service to local control. According to Ouchi, the money must follow the child. The only true local control occurs when the principal controls the school budget.

At John Hay Elementary School in Seattle, which Ouchi profiled, the principal controlled about $25,000 a year before decentralization and now controls about $2 million. The principal used her new freedom to hire 12 part-time reading and math coaches and set up a tutoring station outside every classroom, plus another station in a wide hallway, for "turbo-tutoring" the gifted children. Now the school teaches reading in groups of five to seven students while other classes are in larger sections, and every student who is behind grade level receives one-on-one tutoring. During a four-year period following the change, the school's standardized math scores rose from the 36th percentile to the 62nd, and reading scores rose from the 72nd percentile to the 76th. In third grade, black and white students now have identical reading scores, and all of them are at or above grade level.

Such gains also occur in other districts that have implemented public school choice and the weighted student formula. After Oakland's first year of student-based budgeting, a majority of the city's African-American students met basic reading standards at their grade levels in 2005—probably a first in recent district history. In addition, every grade level in Oakland saw increases in the number of students who were proficient in reading and math. Similarly, in 2005 Cincinnati public schools, where 70 percent of students are African-American, improved their state rating from "Academic Watch" to "Continuous Improvement," and test scores were up for most students in most grade levels. Seattle also continues to see increases in student achievement and in 2005 reduced the number of schools rated "failing" under the No Child Left Behind Act from 20 to 18, even as the state raised the bar for proficiency.

As a result of these changes, parents are returning to public schools. In Seattle, the public school district has won back 8 percent of all students from the private schools since implementing the new system. In Edmonton, where it all began, the public schools are so popular that there are no private schools left. Three of the largest private schools voluntarily became public schools and joined the Edmonton district. (This has not held true in San Francisco, where families continue to leave the city, largely because of high housing costs. San Francisco's private schools have lost enrollment as well, as the city's child population reaches an all-time low of 11 percent.)

School Choice Free
of Government Restraints

Public school choice is not a panacea. In many districts there have been tensions between parents who want more choices and parents who want their children to have a guaranteed spot in a neighborhood school. In Seattle, the district recently considered abolishing the school choice system in favor of the traditional system based on a child's address. The district's reasoning is that busing students all over Seattle is complicated and expensive. So far, a parental outcry has staved off the plans to return to residence-based schools. Parents have suggested charging for transportation or leaving it up to families rather than killing off school choice.

In addition, unlike an actual market system in education, public schools are still strapped with myriad local, state, and federal regulations. No matter how decentralized San Francisco schools become, they still must comply with the No Child Left Behind Act and abide by silly state laws, such as the California statute that forbids parents from bringing home-baked cupcakes to school to celebrate their children's birthdays with classmates.

Public school choice is at best a weak substitute for true school choice, where parents are not bound by excessive government regulations. In support of this point, Ouchi's research found that the three Catholic school systems he examined—Chicago, New York City, and Los Angeles—were the most decentralized. They have very small central staffs, spend the least money per pupil, and have the highest student achievement. (While demographics do not affect the per-pupil spending or smaller centralized staff in Catholic schools, they probably contribute to higher test scores. For example, the New York City Catholic schools in Ouchi's study have only 32 percent low-income children, compared to 74 in the city's public schools.)

Ouchi's findings reinforce the main criticism of decentralized public schools: Is it really necessary to stay within the bounds of the existing public school system and complete the difficult task of changing the system from within? A better alternative would be to move to a direct financing mechanism through vouchers, tax credits, or charter schools—an arrangement under which per-pupil funding immediately empowers parents and leads to the most decentralized schools of all, with 100 percent local budget control.

The Best Option Within the Public School System

Yet the better alternative is not always the politically feasible alternative. School decentralization offers a compelling model for restructuring school financing, giving principals and parents true control over their schools, and offering real school choice to all students within the constraints of a public school system. It also gets parents used to the idea that schools need not be linked to real estate. And it demonstrates that even within a limited pseudo-market, when families become consumers of education services with the right of exit, schools quickly improve to attract them.

The San Francisco parents I spoke with probably would be alarmed by the market metaphor. In general, these parents do not support education tax credits or school vouchers. They are for public education. Yet San Francisco has adopted a school district financing system that mimics a school market and has led to a revitalization of the city's public schools. And these parents have taken full advantage.

Caroline Grannan admits she probably could have worked the old residential assignment system to get her kids into good schools. But times have changed in the City by the Bay. When Grannan's son William was applying for high schools, she was one of many middle-class parents now willing to send her child to Balboa High School, which not long ago was

257

viewed as a low-performing, dangerous "ghetto school." William ended up going to SOTA, the School of the Arts, to which students are admitted by audition. But as Grannan says, "Knowing that we were fine with Balboa if he hadn't gotten into SOTA made the entire process much lower-stress." The difference, she says, is "the comfort in knowing that parents have more than one option."

Periodical Bibliography

The following articles have been selected to supplement the diverse views presented in this chapter.

| Bruce Buchanan | "Beyond the Basics," *American School Board Journal*, May 2008. |

| Nora Carr | "The Pay-for-Performance Pitfall," *American School Board Journal*, February 2008. |

| Linda Darling-Hammond | "How They Do It Abroad," *Time*, February 25, 2008. |

| Sam Dillon | "Imported from Britain: Ideas to Improve Schools," *New York Times*, August 15, 2007. |

| Sam Dillon | "Online Schooling Grows, Setting off Debate," *New York Times*, February 1, 2008. |

| John Merrow | "The Influence of Teachers," *Independent School*, Winter 2008. |

| Josh Patashnik | "Reform School," *New Republic*, March 26, 2008. |

| Stephanie Perrin | "Why Arts Education Matters," *Education Week*, January 30, 2008. |

| Phillip C. Schlechty | "No Community Left Behind," *Phi Delta Kappan*, April 2008. |

| Emma Smith | "Raising Standards in American Schools? Problems with Improving Teacher Quality," *Teaching & Teacher Education*, April 2008. |

| Kenneth A. Strike | "Small Schools: Size or Community?" *American Journal of Education*, May 2008. |

| Claudia Wallis, et al. | "How to Make Great Teachers," *Time*, February 25, 2008. |

| Joel Westheimer | "No Child Left Thinking," *Independent School*, Spring 2008. |

For Further Discussion

Chapter 1

1. Tom DeWeese contends that the American education system no longer educates students in the academic subjects needed to succeed and compete in the world today. Mike Rose, on the other hand, states that arguments decrying the poor state of the education system ignore the daily accomplishments of the system and do not help to foster meaningful improvement. Whose argument do you find more convincing, and which one coincides more with your experiences with the American education system? Explain your answer.

2. Both Bobbie A. Solley and Linda Crocker cite extensive research to support their viewpoints on the impact of standardized testing on the American education system. Does this tactic strengthen their arguments? Which author more effectively utilizes prior studies to support her opinion? Use examples from the texts to support your answer.

3. In the *Brown v. Board of Education* case of 1954, the United States Supreme Court ruled that separate-but-equal laws allowing segregation in public schools were unconstitutional. In 2007 the Supreme Court ruled that public school programs that voluntarily desegregate schools are likewise unconstitutional. After reading the viewpoint by Theodore M. Shaw and Lee C. Bollinger in favor of the continued use of *Brown* mandates and the viewpoint by Juan Williams who argues that the guidelines of *Brown* are outdated and should be abandoned, do you think ending desegregation practices will help or harm America's public schools? Conduct additional research on the history of *Brown v. Board of Education* and find additional articles to support your view.

Chapter 2

1. Referring to the viewpoints by Mark Harrison and John F. Covaleskie, as well as the opinions expressed in the introduction to this anthology, explain whether you think privatizing education is a worthwhile means of rescuing disadvantaged schools. Be sure to list the advantages that you deem important and include reasons why you think the opposing views do not address the needs of students in these schools.

2. Elena Silva asserts that same-sex schooling would be a setback for gender equality. Explain how Silva makes this argument and then decide whether you agree with her views.

Chapter 3

1. After reading the viewpoint by Charles C. Haynes and Marvin W. Berkowitz and the viewpoint by Bobby Ann Starnes, explain whether you think schools should devote part of their curriculum to teaching character development. If you believe that character should be taught in schools, explain how you think it can be incorporated into lesson plans without becoming condescending, as Starnes argues. If you do not advocate character education in schools, explain how you would counter absenteeism, student motivation, and the other problems Haynes and Berkowitz see as plaguing schools.

2. After reviewing the articles on evolution and intelligent design, make an argument for or against teaching intelligent design in school. If you favor teaching intelligent design, in which class should it be taught? Explain how it should be taught. If you disagree with the teaching of intelligent design, explain why you would bar it from classroom discussion.

3. Lucas Carpenter asserts that a liberal education should be based on skepticism, scientific investigation, and objective

knowledge. Examine Carpenter's claim and explain whether you agree with his argument or whether you believe a liberal education should include other types of learning (and define what those unnamed aspects are).

Chapter 4

1. School accountability is an often-proposed solution to improve education in the United States. Proponents of plans such as No Child Left Behind, charter schools, and decentralized schools all believe that these plans will improve education by shutting down schools that are not performing well and rewarding those schools that produce results. Opponents of these plans argue that accountability will not lead to better education for American students. The first and last pairs of articles in this chapter discuss the issue of accountability. Based on these readings, do you think that holding schools and teachers accountable for the success of their students will improve education in the United States? Which plans for accountability do you think are the most likely to produce results, or are accountability programs even appropriate in the education system? Use specific examples from the articles to support your view.

2. Frederick M. Hess believes that compensatory pay for teachers based on experience and results will improve education by providing capable individuals with incentives for excelling in the teaching field. Reg Weaver and Dave Riegel contend that paying teachers based on experience and results is unfair and that these methods of determining pay will increase competition between teachers, thus hampering the education process. Whose argument do you find more convincing? Why? Do you believe that paying teachers based on performance helps or harms education?

Organizations to Contact

The editors have compiled the following list of organizations concerned with the issues debated in this book. The descriptions are derived from materials provided by the organizations. All have publications or information available for interested readers. The list was compiled on the date of publication of the present volume; the information provided here may change. Be aware that many organizations take several weeks or longer to respond to inquiries, so allow as much time as possible.

American Enterprise Institute (AEI)
1150 Seventeenth Street NW, Washington, DC   20036
(202) 862-5800 • fax: (202) 862-7177
Web site: www.aei.org

The American Enterprise Institute (AEI) is a conservative public policy institute that provides research and educational materials on social, political, and economic issues in the United States. The institute promotes policies that advocate limited government, private enterprise, individual liberty, and a vigilant defense and foreign policy. With regards to education, AEI scholars focus their work on assessing all aspects of the American education system and the need for reform with an emphasis on topics such as school financing and parental choice, the No Child Left Behind Act, accountability in education, and teacher education and certification. Articles on these topics and others can be found on the institute's Web site and in AEI's bimonthly magazine, *The American.*

American Policy Center (APC)
70 Main Street, Suite 23, Warrenton, VA   20186
(540) 341-8911 • fax: (540) 341-8917
e-mail: ampolicycenter@hotmail.com
Web site: www.americanpolicy.org

The American Policy Center (APC) is a grass roots organization committed to promoting free enterprise and limited government regulations in both commerce and individual life. The center contends that the free market provides the best opportunities for individuals and the United States as a country to realize their full potential. APC argues against increased federal involvement in the U.S. education system because it believes that the federal government's management of public education has not benefited American students. Articles outlining current problems and possible solutions for education in America can be found on the APC Web site as well as in the monthly publication of the organization, *The DeWeese Report.*

Center for Character & Citizenship

402 Marillac Hall, One University Boulevard
St. Louis, MO   63121-4499
(314) 516-7521 • fax: (314) 516-7356
e-mail: ccc@umsl.edu
Web site: www.characterandcitizenship.org

The Center for Character & Citizenship is an organization within the University of Missouri's College of Education at St. Louis that provides scholars, educators, and organizations with information about the development of moral and civic character and the tools needed to foster these traits in students. The center publishes the *Journal of Research in Character Education* as well as individual reports such as *What Works in Character Education: A Research-Driven Guide for Educators.* Articles from the journal, copies of center reports, and additional resources can all be accessed on the center's Web site.

Center on Education Policy (CEP)

1001 Connecticut Avenue NW, Suite 522
Washington, DC   20036
(202) 822-8065 • fax: (202) 822-6008
e-mail: cep-dc@cep-dc.org
Web site: www.cep-dc.org

The Center on Education Policy (CEP) is a national, independent organization dedicated to promoting and improving public schools. The organization works on national, state, and local levels to inform the government and the public about the importance of the public education system through its publications, meetings, and presentations. Reports on issues regarding all aspects of the education system, such as federal education programs, testing, vouchers, and ways to improve public schools, can be found on the CEP Web site.

Center for Education Reform (CER)
910 Seventeenth Street NW, Suite 1120
Washington, DC   20006
(800) 521-2118 • fax: (301) 986-1826
e-mail: cer@edreform.com
Web site: www.edreform.com

The Center for Education Reform (CER) is a grassroots, educational policy organization that advocates for education reform policies that ensure high standards, accountability, and school choice. The organization argues that policies creating more charter schools and educational choice scholarships will improve education in the United States. The CER Web site offers numerous articles on issues such as charter schools, school choice, curriculum, and teacher related issues.

Character Education Partnership (CEP)
1025 Connecticut Avenue NW, Suite 1011
Washington, DC   20036
(800) 988-8081 • fax: (202) 296-7779
Web site: www.character.org

Character Education Partnership (CEP) works nationally to promote the value and need for character education in all of America's schools. CEP believes that character education, which focuses on educating students in ethics, responsibility, and caring, is essential to creating well-rounded citizens in society at large and within the education system. CEP publishes annual reports assessing the status of character education in the United States, and also provides online resources such as *CEP's Eleven Principles of Effective Character Education* and *Character Education Quality Standards* which outline effective character education programs.

Discovery Institute

208 Columbia Street, Seattle, WA 98104

(206) 292-0401 • fax: (206) 682-5320

e-mail: info@discovery.org

Web site: www.discovery.org

Discovery Institute promotes the ideas of a representative government, the free market, and individual liberty through its books, reports, legislative testimony, and conferences. Specifically, the institute investigates areas such as technology, science and culture, and religion and public life. The Center for Science and Culture (CSC) is the Discovery Institute's program aimed specifically at challenging neo-Darwinian theory and advancing the alternative theory of intelligent design. The CSC Web site contains archives of articles and research on intelligent design, "teaching the controversy" of evolution, and other aspects of the intelligent design vs. evolution debate.

Education Commission of the States (ECS)

700 Broadway, No. 810, Denver, CO 80203-3442

(303) 299-3600 • fax: (303) 296-8332

e-mail: ecs@ecs.org

Web site: www.ecs.org

The Education Commission of the States (ECS) is an organization comprised of forty-nine states, three territories, and the District of Columbia that works to improve the quality of public schools nationwide. The organization provides a forum for educators and policymakers to share ideas and experiences. ECS provides policy research and analysis on current educational issues, sponsors state, regional, and national policy conferences, and publishes four bimonthly bulletins: *Citizenship Matters*, *Governance Notes*, *Leadership Links*, and *TQ Update*, each addressing specific topics in education policy. The ECS Web site provides a comprehensive list of education-related issues with overviews, fact sheets, and additional information about each.

The Friedman Foundation for Educational Choice

One American Square, Suite 2420, Indianapolis, IN 46282
(317) 681-0745 • fax: (317) 681-0945
Web site: www.friendmanfoundation.org

The Friedman Foundation for Education Choice was founded in 1996 to advance the idea that quality elementary and secondary schools will emerge if parents are given the freedom to choose the schools that are most appropriate for their children. The foundation believes that the quality of education in the United States will improve only if the education system is reformed using the free market ideals of choice and competition. *ABCs of School Choice* is the annual report published by the foundation providing information on the current status of school choice in the United States, and *The School Choice Advocate* is the organization's periodic magazine. Additional reports and articles can be found on the Friedman Foundation Web site.

The Heritage Foundation

214 Massachusetts Avenue NE, Washington, DC 20002-4999
(202) 546-4400 • fax: (202) 546-8328
e-mail: info@heritage.org
Web site: www.heritage.org

The Heritage Foundation is a conservative public policy organization dedicated to promoting policies that align with the principles of free enterprise, limited government, individual freedom, traditional American values, and a strong national defense. The Heritage Foundation believes that good governance on the state, not the federal, level and giving parents the power to choose the right school for their children are the best methods for improving education in the Untied States. The foundation's Web site provides topical articles on these and other issues.

National Alliance for Public Charter Schools
1101 Fourteenth Street NW, Washington, DC   20005
(202) 289-2700 • fax: (202) 289-4009
Web site: www.publiccharters.org

The National Alliance for Public Charter Schools works to develop policies in support of public charter school access for those who cannot afford more expensive alternatives to public schools. The alliance also works to increase public and political knowledge and support of the charter school model of education so that a wider variety and larger number of students are able to benefit from the advantages charters schools offer. Many publications outlining these advantages and focusing on what needs to be done to improve education in the United States can be accessed on the organization's Web site.

National Association for Single Sex Public Education (NASSPE)
PO Box 108, 19710 Fisher Avenue, Suite J
Poolesville, MD   20837
(301) 461-5065 • fax: (301) 972-8006
e-mail: contact@singlesexschools.org
Web site: www.singlesexschools.org

The National Association for Single Sex Public Education (NASSPE) is a nonprofit organization that promotes the value and adoption of a single-sex educational model in the nation's public schools. The organization provides research supporting the implementation of single-sex programs for both boys and girls; educates teachers, parents, and administrators about the benefits of single-sex schools; and offers professional development programs for teachers to share single-sex teaching strategies. NASSPE's Web site provides articles and research, recommended readings, and links to other sites supporting single-sex schools.

The National Center for Fair & Open Testing (FairTest)
342 Broadway, Cambridge, MA   02139
(617) 864-4810 • fax: (617) 497-2224

Web site: www.fairtest.org

FairTest is an organization that seeks to ensure that all students receive a quality education and equal opportunity through the use of appropriate evaluations of students, teachers, and schools. Additionally, the organization works to eradicate the misuse of testing that hinders the education system. Specifically, FairTest focuses its efforts on eliminating racial, class, gender, and cultural barriers that can emerge with the use of standardized testing. *The Examiner* is the regular electronic newsletter of FairTest; additional fact sheets and reports can be found on the organization's Web site.

National Center for Science Education (NCSE)
420 Fortieth Street, Suite 2, Oakland, CA   94609-2509
(510) 601-7203 • fax: (510) 601-7204
e-mail: ncseoffice@ncseweb.org
Web site: www.natcenscied.org

The National Center for Science Education (NCSE) is a non-profit, membership organization dedicated to continuing the teaching of evolution in public school science education classrooms. The center provides information and resources for schools, parents, and the press about the importance of teaching evolution as well as the legal aspects of the creation vs. evolution controversy. Archived *Reports of the National Center for Science Education*, the bimonthly journal of the NCSE, can be viewed online in addition to other resources and reports.

National Council on Measurement in Education (NCME)
2810 Crossroads Drive, Suite 3800, Madison, WI   53718
(608) 443-2487 • fax: (608) 443-2474
Web site: www.ncme.org

The National Council on Measurement in Education (NCME) works to advance and improve the science of measurement in the education field in order to make assessment a more useful tool in the movement to improve education in the United States. NCME publishes the quarterly *Journal of Education Measurement* and the quarterly *Educational Measurement: Issues and Practice.*

National Education Association (NEA)

1201 Sixteenth Street NW, Washington, DC   20036-3290

(202) 833-4000 • fax: (202) 822-7974

Web site: www.nea.org

The National Education Association (NEA) is a professional employee organization open to any employee of public schools, colleges, and universities. On the local level, NEA volunteers and affiliate organizations work in a variety of capacities, from raising funds for scholarship programs to bargaining contracts for school district employees. At both the state and national level, NEA affiliates lobby legislators on behalf of its members and public schools in an effort to protect academic freedom, ensure the rights of school employees, and increase the effectiveness of public education. Among other stances, NEA opposes vouchers, supports the use of professional pay to recruit and retain quality teachers, and works to ensure that the achievement gap of low-income and minority students is reduced. *NEA Today* is the monthly magazine of the NEA.

Progressive Policy Institute (PPI)

600 Pennsylvania Avenue SE, Suite 400

Washington, DC   20003

(202) 547-0001 • fax: (202) 544-5014

Web site: www.ppionline.org

The Progressive Policy Institute (PPI) works to define and promote progressive public policy through its research, policies, and education; it is a project of the Third Way, a global movement seeking to modernize progressive politics in the information age. In the area of education, the institute focuses its research on improving teacher quality, increasing school choice, strengthening accountability, and expanding the implementation of innovative strategies in public education. Articles outlining the institute's stances on these educational topics and others can be found on the PPI Web site.

United States Department of Education (ED)

400 Maryland Avenue SW, Washington, DC 20202
(800) 872-5327
Web site: www.ed.gov

The United State Department of Education (ED) was established by Congress on May 4, 1980, with the goal of improving education nationwide through the use of federally mandated education programs. Initiatives by ED have focused on increasing the accountability of public schools and teachers, as well as providing research and evaluation on school issues. ED publishes a variety of newsletters on specific topics relating to education; all of these and other publications and reports by the department can be accessed online.

Bibliography of Books

John Charles
Boger and Gary
Orfield

School Resegregation: Must the South Turn Back? Chapel Hill: University of North Carolina Press, 2005.

Gerald W. Bracey

On the Death of Childhood and the Destruction of Public Schools: The Folly of Today's Education Policies and Practices. Portsmouth, NH: Heinemann, 2003.

Evans Clinchy

Rescuing the Public Schools: What It Will Take to Leave No Child Behind. New York: Teachers College Press, 2007.

Ronald G.
Corwin and E.
Joseph Schneider

The School Choice Hoax: Fixing America's Schools. Westport, CT: Praeger, 2005.

William Damon,
ed.

Bringing in a New Era in Character Education. Stanford, CA: Hoover Institution, 2002.

Richard F. Elmore

School Reform from the Inside Out: Policy, Practice, and Performance. Cambridge, MA: Harvard Education Press, 2004.

Kathy Emery and
Susan Ohanian

Why Is Corporate America Bashing Our Public Schools? Portsmouth, NH: Heinemann, 2004.

Norm Fruchter

Urban Schools, Public Will: Making Education Work for All Our Children. New York: Teachers College Press, 2007.

Carl Glickman, ed. *Letters to the Next President: What We Can Do About the Real Crisis in Public Education.* New York: Teachers College Press, 2007.

Ken Goodman, et al. *Saving Our Schools: The Case for Public Education, Saying No to "No Child Left Behind."* Berkeley, CA: RDR, 2004.

Jay P. Greene *Education Myths: What Special Interest Groups Want You to Believe About Our Schools—And Why It Isn't So.* Lanham, MD: Rowman & Littlefield, 2005.

Frederick M. Hess *Common Sense School Reform.* New York: Palgrave Macmillan, 2004.

Frederick M. Hess and Chester E. Finn Jr., eds. *Leaving No Child Behind?: Options for Kids in Failing Schools.* New York: Palgrave Macmillan, 2004.

H. Wayne House, ed. *Intelligent Design 101: Leading Experts Explain the Key Issues.* Grand Rapids, MI: Kregel, 2008.

Myron S. Kayes and Robert Maranto, eds. *A Guide to Charter Schools: Research and Practical Advice for Educators.* Lanham, MD: Rowman & Littlefield, 2006.

Alfie Kohn *The Case Against Standardized Testing: Raising the Scores, Ruining the Schools.* Portsmouth, NH: Heinemann, 2000.

Jonathan Kozol   *The Shame of the Nation: The Restoration of Apartheid Schooling in America.* New York: Crown, 2005.

Marlin Maddoux   *Public Education Against America: The Hidden Agenda.* New Kensington, PA: Whitaker House, 2006.

Deborah Meier   *In Schools We Trust: Creating Communities of Learning in an Era of Testing and Standardization.* Boston, MA: Beacon, 2002.

Deborah Meier and George Wood, eds.   *Many Children Left Behind: How the No Child Left Behind Act Is Damaging Our Children and Our Schools.* Boston, MA: Beacon, 2004.

Paul E. Peterson and Martin R. West, eds.   *No Child Left Behind?: The Politics and Practice of School Accountability.* Washington, DC: Brookings Institution, 2003.

Andrew J. Petto and Laurie R. Godfrey, eds.   *Scientists Confront Intelligent Design and Creationism.* New York: W.W. Norton & Co., 2007.

Richard P. Phelps, ed.   *Defending Standardized Testing.* Mahwah, NJ: L. Erlbaum Associates, 2005.

Richard P. Phelps   *Kill the Messenger: The War on Standardized Testing.* New Brunswick, NJ: Transaction, 2003.

Diane Ravitch   *Left Back: A Century of Failed School Reforms.* New York: Simon & Schuster, 2000.

William J. Reese — *America's Public Schools: From the Common School to "No Child Left Behind."* Baltimore, MD: Johns Hopkins University Press, 2005.

Peter Sacks — *Standardized Minds: The High Price of America's Testing Culture and What We Can Do to Change It.* Cambridge, MA: Perseus, 1999.

Rosemary C. Salomone — *Same, Different, Equal: Rethinking Single-Sex Schooling.* New Haven, CT: Yale University Press, 2003.

Karen Stabiner — *All Girls: Single-Sex Education and Why It Matters.* New York: Riverhead, 2002.

Charles J. Sykes — *Dumbing Down Our Kids: Why American Children Feel Good About Themselves But Can't Read, Write, or Add.* New York: St. Martins, 1996.

Beverly Daniel Tatum — *Can We Talk About Race?: And Other Conversations in an Era of School Resegregation.* Boston, MA: Beacon, 2007.

Joel Turtel — *Public Schools, Public Menace: How Public Schools Lie to Parents and Betray Our Children.* Staten Island, NY: Liberty, 2005.

Herbert J. Walberg — *School Choice: The Findings.* Washington, DC: Cato Institute, 2007.

Joe Williams — *Cheating Our Kids: How Politics and Greed Ruin Education.* New York: Palgrave Macmillan, 2005.

Bob Wise

Raising the Grade: How High School Reform Can Save Our Youth and Our Nation. San Francisco: Jossey-Bass, 2008.

Alan Wolfe, ed.

School Choice: The Moral Debate. Princeton, NJ: Princeton University Press, 2003.

Index